EXPANDED

POWER AND
TERROR

Conflict, Hegemony,
and the Rule of Force

NOAM CHOMSKY

Edited by John Junkerman
and Takei Masakazu

Parts of this book were originally published in association with the theatrical release of *Power and Terror: Noam Chomsky in Our Times*, a film by John Junkerman, produced by Siglo, Ltd., Tokyo; Yamagami Tetsujiro, producer. Distributed in North America by First Run Features. www.firstrunfeatures.com

It was first published as *Noam Chomsky*, by Little More, Tokyo, September 2002, in association with the release of the original Japanese version of the film (Japanese title: *Chomsky 9.11*). The first English-language edition, *Power and Terror: Post-9/11 Talks and Interviews*, was published in 2003 by Seven Stories Press.

First published in the United Kingdom by Pluto Press
345 Archway Road, London N6 5AA
www.plutobooks.com

This new book includes additional selections made by Noam Chomsky and Paradigm Publishers (Part IV) to further update the book.

British Library Cataloguing in Publication Data
A catalogue record for this book is available from the British Library.

ISBN 978-0-7453-3137-9 (paperback : alk. paper)

10   9   8   7   6   5   4   3   2

Designed and Typeset by Straight Creek Bookmakers in Trump Medieval.
Printed in the European Union by CPI Antony Rowe, Chippenham and Eastbourne.

CONTENTS

Foreword

NOAM CHOMSKY IS AMERICA'S GREATEST intellectual. His massive body of work, which includes nearly 100 books, has for decades deflated and exposed the lies of the power elite, the myths they perpetrate, and the complicity of a duplicitous liberal class. Chomsky has done this despite being blacklisted by the commercial media, ignored by academics that he towers above, and turned into a pariah. His influence as a thinker comes from his marriage of moral autonomy with rigorous and exacting scholarship. He has a stunning grasp of detail, a deep understanding of the nature of power and language as well as a remarkable talent to synthesize information into withering and prescient social and political critiques. He correctly dismisses our two-party system as a mirage orchestrated by the corporate state. He excoriates the liberal class for being weak and complicit in the corporate demolition of the country. He describes the drivel of the commercial media as a form of "brainwashing." And as our nation's most prescient critic of unregulated capitalism, globalization, and the poison of empire, he warns us that we have little time left to save our anemic democracy.

The book *Power and Terror* is Chomsky at his best. He demonstrates his ability in these interviews and lectures to stand in the shoes of those outside our gates and ask the uncomfortable moral questions that should be asked. He excoriates U.S. intellectuals for blindly supporting the bombing in Afghanistan and correctly asks how many of these same intellectuals would have supported bombing Washington because of the U.S. wars against Nicaragua or Cuba. This is vintage Chomsky. Chomsky believes passionately in justice and the rule of law. The standards we apply to others should, he argues, also be applied to us. And this simple demand—that the rule of law be followed—is in the world of foreign policy, and especially our relations with Israel, a radical and unheard of stance. It challenges the assumed moral superiority that has infected the power elite and our intellectual class of mandarins and courtiers, many of whom drift from the university to government and back again. Chomsky has none of it. He exposes a crime as a crime.

"Unpopular ideas can be suppressed without the use of force," Chomsky warns, "and a good education is an effective means to reach this result. Well, unless we can become capable of thinking the thoughts that are banned by imperial ideology, understanding of what's happening in the world is going to be very difficult to attain."

Chomsky has likened our decayed state to that of Weimar Germany. He points to the widespread apathy and disillusionment with electoral politics and the failure of traditional liberals to advance basic liberal values, serving instead the crushing demands of the corporate state. He warns that the growing distaste for the traditional parties here, as in Weimar Germany, opens up a space that radical groups and the lunatic fringe of the political landscape are beginning to fill.

"The United States is extremely lucky that no honest, charismatic figure has arisen," Chomsky told me. "Every charismatic figure is such an obvious crook that he destroys himself, like McCarthy or Nixon or the evangelist preachers. If somebody comes along who is charismatic and honest, this country is in real trouble because of the frustration, disillusionment, the justified anger, and the absence of any coherent response. What are people supposed to think if someone says 'I have got an answer, we have an enemy'? There it was the Jews. Here it will be the illegal immigrants and the blacks. We will be told that white males are a persecuted minority. We will be told we have to defend ourselves and the honor of the nation. Military force will be exalted. People will be beaten up. This could become an overwhelming force. And if it happens it will be more dangerous than Germany. The United States is the world power. Germany was powerful but had more powerful antagonists. I don't think all this is very far away. If the polls are accurate it is not the Republicans but the right-wing Republicans, the crazed Republicans, who will sweep the next election."

"I have never seen anything like this in my lifetime," Chomsky added. "I am old enough to remember the 1930s. My whole family was unemployed. There were far more desperate conditions than today. But it was hopeful. People had hope. The CIO was organizing. No one wants to say it anymore but the Communist Party was the spearhead for labor and civil rights organizing. Even things like giving my unemployed seamstress aunt a week in the country. It was a life. There is nothing like that now. The mood of the country is frightening. The level of anger, frustration, and hatred of institutions is not organized in a constructive way. It is going off into self-destructive fantasies."

"I listen to talk radio," Chomsky said. "I don't want to hear Rush Limbaugh. I want to hear the people calling in. They are like Joe Stack. What is happening to me? I have done all the right things. I am a God-fearing Christian. I work hard for my family. I have a gun. I believe in the values of the country and my life is collapsing."

Chomsky has, more than any other American intellectual, followed the downward spiral of the American political and economic systems, in works such as *On Power and Ideology* and *Manufacturing Consent.* He reminds us that genuine intellectual inquiry is always subversive. It challenges cultural and political assumptions. It critiques structures. It is relentlessly self-critical. It implodes the self-indulgent myths and stereotypes we use to elevate ourselves and ignore our complicity in acts of violence and oppression. And it always makes the powerful, as well as their liberal apologists, deeply uncomfortable.

Chomsky reserves his fiercest venom for the liberal class who serve as a smoke screen for the cruelty of unchecked capitalism and imperial war. He has consistently exposed their moral and intellectual posturing as a fraud. And this is why Chomsky is hated, and perhaps feared, more among liberals than among the right wing he also excoriates. When Christopher Hitchens decided to become a windup doll for the Bush administration after 9/11, one of the first things he did was write a vicious article attacking Chomsky. Hitchens, unlike most of the warmongers he served, knew which intellectual in America mattered.

"I don't bother writing about Fox News," Chomsky said when we spoke. "It is too easy. What I talk about are the liberal intellectuals, the ones who portray themselves and perceive themselves as challenging power, as courageous, as standing up for truth and justice. They are basically the guardians of the faith. They set the limits. They tell us how far we can go. They say, 'Look how courageous I am.' But do not go one millimeter beyond that. At least for the educated sectors, they are the most dangerous in supporting power." Chomsky, because he steps outside of every group and eschews all ideologies, has been crucial to American discourse for decades, from his work on the Vietnam War to his criticisms of the Obama administration. He stubbornly maintains his position as an iconoclast, one who distrusts power in any form. And he is one of the few voices that speak to the reality of war, the disastrous effects of imperial power and the fact that, rather than promoting virtue or waging war based on good intentions, the permanent war economy is consuming and destroying hundreds of thousands of innocent lives. Chomsky understands that to speak morally one must always be alienated from systems of power, no matter what their ideological stripe. He sees two sets of principles that are at odds with each other. The first is power and privilege. The second is truth and justice. Those, like Chomsky, who vigorously pursue truth and justice, are despised by those who seek privilege and power. And the traditional liberal class, positing itself as the conscience of the nation while also seeking access to privileged and power, detests Chomsky because he exposes to public view their hypocrisy and duplicity. The liberals, the ones who call themselves "reluctant hawks" and support war as the only valid moral choice, illustrate the deceitful game most in the liberal class play. These liberals, columnists such as Thomas Friedman or Michael Ignatieff, currently the Canadian Liberal Party leader, seek at once to appease the powerbrokers they serve and yet claim for themselves the virtues they have betrayed. Chomsky will have none of it.

"Some of Chomsky's books will consist of things like analyzing the misrepresentations of the Arias plan in Central America, and he will devote 200 pages to it," the Middle East scholar Norman Finkelstein said when we spoke about Chomsky. "And two years later, who will have heard of Oscar Arias? It causes you to wonder would Chomsky have been wiser to write things on a grander scale, things with a more enduring quality so that you read them forty or sixty years later. This is what Russell did in books like *Marriage and Morals.* Can you even read any longer what Chomsky wrote on Vietnam and Central America? The answer has to often be no. This tells you something about him. He is not writing for ego. If he were writing for ego, he would have written in a grand style that would have buttressed his legacy. He is writing because he wants to effect political change. He cares about the lives of people and there the details count. He is trying to refute the daily lies spewed out by the establishment media. He could have devoted his time to writing philosophical treatises that would have endured like Kant or Russell. But he invested in the tiny details which make a difference to win a political battle."

"I try to encourage people to think for themselves, to question standard assumptions," Chomsky said when I asked about his goals. "Don't take assumptions for granted. Begin by taking a skeptical attitude toward anything that is conventional wisdom. Make it justify itself. It usually can't. Be willing to ask questions about what is taken for granted. Try to think things through for yourself. There is plenty of information. You have got to learn how to judge, evaluate and compare it with other things. You have to take some things on trust or you can't survive. But if there is something significant and important, don't take it on trust. As soon as you read anything that is anonymous, you should immediately distrust it. If you read in the newspapers that Iran is defying the international community, ask who is the international community? India is opposed to sanctions. China is opposed to sanctions. Brazil is opposed to sanctions. The Non-Aligned Movement is vigorously opposed to sanctions and has been for years. Who is the international community? It is Washington and anyone who happens to agree with it. You can figure that out, but you have to do work. It is the same on issue after issue."

Chomsky's courage to speak on behalf of those whose suffering is minimized or ignored in mass culture, especially the Palestinians, holds up the possibility of the moral life. And, perhaps even more than his scholarship, his example of intellectual and moral independence sustains all those who defy the cant of systems of power to speak the truth.

"I cannot tell you how many people, myself included, and this is not hyperbole, whose lives were changed by him," said Finkelstein, who, like Chomsky, has been ridiculed and ignored because of his intellectual courage and independence. "Were it not for Chomsky, I would have long ago succumbed. I was beaten and battered in my professional life. It was only the knowledge that one of the greatest minds in human history has faith in me that compensates for this constant, relentless, and vicious battering. There are many people who are considered nonentities, the so-called little people of this world, who suddenly get an email from Noam Chomsky. It breathes new life into you. Chomsky has stirred many, many people to realize a level of their potential that would forever have been lost."

Introduction

IMMEDIATELY AFTER THE TERRORIST ATTACKS of
September 11, Noam Chomsky's always tightly scheduled
life ratcheted several levels higher in intensity. In the
months that followed, he gave a great many public talks
and countless interviews, many of them with the foreign
media, who turned to him as one of the small handful of
American intellectuals who stood opposed to the Bush administration's aggressive military response to the attacks.

With unflagging conviction, Chomsky must have
repeated a thousand times his argument that we cannot
address terrorism of the weak against the powerful without also confronting "the unmentionable but far more
extreme terrorism of the powerful against the weak."
The argument, supported with an ever-expanding array of historical case studies, documents, and analyses,
fell on deaf ears in Washington and in the mainstream
American media, but resonated with large audiences in
the United States and abroad who turned once again to
Chomsky for the voice of reason and conscience that he
has provided for decades.

Chomsky's voice also reached Japan, where I live, in the
form of a translation of his book *9-11* (subtitled in Japanese,

"America Is Not Qualified to Retaliate!"), which was rushed into publication at the end of November. Inspired by the book, a producer at an independent Japanese film company and I began to make plans to produce a documentary about Chomsky and his perspective on terrorism and American power. This book is an outgrowth of that effort.

We got a quick introduction to the intensity of Chomsky's life when we first approached him about the documentary in early January 2002. He would be interested in working with us on the film, Chomsky said, but the first available slot on his interview schedule was not until May. In the meantime, he'd be traveling to the World Social Forum in Porto Alegre, Brazil; to Turkey to testify at the trial of his Turkish publisher; and to Colombia, as well as spending a week in California in March. We were welcome to join him and film these and any other public talks he gave.

We decided to film in California, where Chomsky had been invited to give two linguistics addresses for an annual lectureship at UC—Berkeley. During his five days in the Bay Area, Chomsky also held office hours on campus and met with linguistics students and faculty in the area; in his "free time," he gave five political talks on an array of topics (three of which we filmed) to a total audience of more than five thousand people.

By the final day, Friday, in Palo Alto, his voice was cracking and he was dead tired, but when he started talking to an intent crowd of one thousand people in a hotel ballroom, he hit his stride. He gained energy as the evening progressed, from a long talk about the threat of space-based missiles into the question-and-answer session—minitalks, really, sometimes ten minutes long, that responded to concerns the audience raised.

After the talk, Chomsky spent another forty-five minutes patiently answering questions from a group of twenty-five who lingered. At one point, his fingers became cramped from signing autographs and he laughed, "I can't even write anymore." Chomsky, the man, may be tireless, but he's not made of steel. He was still talking as he exited the ballroom, telling a friend how inspired he was by his recent trip to the Kurdish region of Turkey.

Following Chomsky during these days, I was struck, first, by his great humility and generosity. He does not see himself as the vehicle for social change but perhaps its enabler, by providing his audience with the information and analysis that are the fruits of his research. He repeatedly emphasizes that there are choices to be made, and that it is up to each individual to act according to moral principle and to force those in power to do the same.

The other thing that struck me was Chomsky's optimism. Despite his often distressing examination of the abuses of American power, Chomsky's disposition is bright and his outlook hopeful. He ends most speeches with a review of how much has been achieved by popular activism over the past several decades and how social change remains well within our grasp.

The Japanese philosopher and activist Tsurumi Shunsuke, who provided editorial supervision for the original Japanese edition of this book, ascribes this optimism to the long view of history provided by Chomsky's study of linguistics. "In the context of that long history, this year and next appear small. Living in the present, with faith in the continuing work of human activity over the span of time—that's where Chomsky's cheerful expression comes from."

Chomsky's work poses the question—and the challenge—to each of us: Is it justified to feel optimistic in this age of smart bombs and jingoistic government? The answer, as Chomsky is wont to say, depends a great deal on what people like you and I decide to do.

John Junkerman
Tokyo
January 2003

Part I

Interview with Noam Chomsky

For the film Power and Terror

This interview by John Junkerman took place in Chomsky's office at the Massachusetts Institute of Technology, Cambridge, on May 21, 2002.

Q: Where were you the day that the event [September 11, 2001] happened? How did you hear about it?

CHOMSKY: I heard about it from a guy I know who is a local workman, works in the area. He had just passed by and told me he had seen it on television. So that's the first I heard.

What was your initial response?

I turned on the radio to find out what was going on, and then obviously, a horrible atrocity. But I reacted pretty much the way people did around the world. A terrible atrocity, but unless you're in Europe or the United States or Japan, I guess, you know it's nothing new. That's the way the imperial powers have treated the rest of the world for hundreds of years. This is a historic event, but unfortunately not because of the scale or the nature of the atrocity but because of who the victims were.

If you look through hundreds of years of history, the imperial countries have been basically immune. There are plenty of atrocities, but they're somewhere else. Like when Japan was carrying out atrocities in China, as far as I'm aware, there were no Chinese terrorist attacks in Tokyo. It's always somewhere else. And that's gone on for hundreds of years. This is the first change.

It's not so surprising. I'd been talking and writing about these things before, and it's in technical literature all over the place. It has been well understood and it's pretty obvious that with contemporary technology, it is possible for small groups without too much technological sophistication to carry out pretty awful atrocities. The gas attack in Japan is an example.[1]

And this kind of thing has been pretty common knowledge, among people who pay any attention, for years. You can find articles in professional journals in the United States well before September 11 that point out that it wouldn't be all that hard to set off a nuclear explosion in New York. There are plenty of loose nuclear weapons around the world, unfortunately, tens of thousands of them and the components for them. There's openly available information on how to put them together to make a small "dirty bomb" or what they call a small bomb, like Hiroshima would be a "small bomb" nowadays. But a Hiroshima bomb in a New York hotel room wouldn't be much fun.

And there would be no problem. I mean, even with very limited capacities, a person could probably sneak things across the Canadian border, which is an unguarded border

and can't be protected. These kinds of things are very likely to happen in the contemporary period, unless the problems are dealt with in a sane fashion. And the sane fashion is to try to figure out where they come from.

It's no use just screaming about it. If you're serious
about trying to prevent further atrocities, you try to find
out what their roots are. And almost any crime, a crime in
the streets, a war, whatever it may be, there's usually
something behind it that has elements of legitimacy, and
you have to consider those elements. That's, again, true
whether it's a crime in the streets or the war crimes of an
aggressive power.

*Some people hear your analysis of this and accuse you of
being an apologist for the terrorists. How do you respond to
that?*

It's the other way around. It's not that I'm apologetic. It's
just a matter of sanity. If you don't care if there are further
terrorist attacks, then fine, say let's not pay any attention
to the reasons. If you're interested in preventing them, of
course you'll pay attention to the reasons. It has nothing
to do with apologetics.

It's very interesting how this criticism works. So, for
example, if I quote the *Wall Street Journal* on reasons that
lie behind the sources for bin Laden–type groups, people
like me will be accused of being apologists, but not the
Wall Street Journal, who I am quoting, which shows you
exactly what is involved. What they're concerned with is
criticism of U.S. policy.

If the material comes from the *Wall Street Journal*, or if

I quote declassified government records that discuss this same problem forty years ago, I'm the apologist, not the National Security Council or the *Wall Street Journal.* Because what they see as the threat is failure to conform and disobedience. But to interpret an effort to find reasons as apologetics is just childish, again, no matter what the crime is.

You mentioned the Hiroshima bomb. We've just recently heard—it's not referred to this way in Japan—that the site of the attack on the World Trade Center is referred to as Ground Zero.

It is.

For Japanese who have experienced the atomic bombs in Nagasaki and Hiroshima, hearing the words "Ground Zero" leads to very complicated feelings. I wondered if you have any thoughts about that.

The interesting thing is that here, almost nobody thinks of it. Check around. I mean, I've never seen a comment in the press or the massive commentary on this that points that out. It's just not in people's consciousness.

But that word...

That's where it comes from, absolutely. No question about it. It struck me right away.

That's why it resonates with people.

I understand. But it doesn't mean that here, because here, it's the same story as before. The atrocities you commit somewhere else don't exist. And that can go on for hundreds of years. I mean, take the United States. Why am I sitting here? Well, I'm sitting here because some religious fundamentalist fanatics from England came over here and started exterminating the local population, and then lots of others followed them and they exterminated the rest of the local population. It wasn't a small affair; it was millions of people.

And the people at the time knew that they were doing it. They didn't have any question about what they were doing. But it's been hundreds of years, and it's just not part of consciousness. In fact, a rather striking fact is that the activism of the 1960s, and the awakening that it led to, brought about a substantial change in this, for the first time in American history. After three hundred years, the question sort of became one that people started thinking about.

When I was growing up as a kid, we played cowboys and Indians. We were the cowboys and we killed the Indians. We never had another thought about it. But that's not true of my children.

Again, with regard to Japan, do you have any thoughts about the Japanese government's participation in the Afghanistan response?

Just about every government bent over backwards to join the U.S.-led coalition, always for their own reasons. So one of the first countries to join with great enthusiasm was Russia. Why Russia? Because they want authorization for pursuing more actively their own horrendous atrocities in Chechnya. China was very happy to join in. They're delighted to have U.S. support for repression in western China. Algeria, one of the biggest terrorist countries in the world, was welcomed into "the coalition against terror."

Maybe the most striking case, the one that really tells you something about Western intellectuals, is Turkey. Turkish troops are now in Kabul, or will be soon, paid for by the United States, to fight the War against Terror. Why is Turkey offering troops? In fact, they were the first country to offer the U.S. troops for Afghanistan, and they explained why. It was in gratitude—because the United States was the only country that was willing to provide them with massive support for their own huge terrorist atrocities in southeast Turkey during the last few years.

It's not ancient history. In fact, it's still going on. They carried out some of the worst atrocities in the 1990s, I mean, far beyond anything that Slobodan Milosevic was accused of in Kosovo, surely before the NATO bombings.

They were carried out at about the same time in southeast Turkey against maybe a quarter of the population, Kurds, who are horribly repressed. And millions of them were driven out of their homes, thousands of villages destroyed, maybe tens of thousands killed, every imaginable kind of barbaric torture.

Clinton was pouring arms in. Turkey became the leading arms recipient in the world outside of Israel and Egypt, which are in a different category. And they're very grateful that the United States was so willing to help them in carrying out massive state terror. And in reward, they are now fighting the "War on Terror." The fact that Western intellectuals can look at this and not say anything is a real impressive testimonial to the discipline of educated people.

In fact, even before September 11, the fiftieth anniversary of NATO in 1999 happened to coincide with the bombing of Serbia. And that was the issue. I mean, isn't this awful? How can we tolerate atrocities so close to the borders of NATO? That was the topic. You couldn't find a word that pointed out that you can not only tolerate such atrocities easily *within* NATO—not across the borders but within NATO—but even make massive contributions to them.

So here's the United States making a massive contribution to huge atrocities within NATO, and at the same time in Washington, the leaders of the Western world are meeting and agonizing over atrocities across the border from NATO, and praising themselves for bombing—what they claim wasn't true—"to prevent the atrocities." And you can't find a word of commentary about that. I wrote about it, but anyone who dared to comment on it was treated as an apologist for Serbian atrocities, just as you mentioned.

Again, this shows incredible discipline. I don't think a totalitarian state could achieve that degree of discipline. It's a rather striking fact about the West. I don't know if anyone in Japan noticed it, but it's extremely dramatic.

Actually, I just had an interview this afternoon with a major German journal and pointed this out, and pointed out to them, which they ought to know, that although the United States was the primary funder of Turkey, Germany was the second. What about that? Everyone's worried about stopping terrorism. Well, there's a really easy way: Stop participating in it. That alone will reduce the amount of terrorism in the world by an enormous quantity.

That's true of just about every country that I know of, to varying degrees, but dramatically true for the United States, Britain, Germany, and others. But that's the way governments react—and intellectuals.

It's an astonishing double standard, or hypocrisy, I suppose. Living in Japan, we often talk about Japanese taking responsibility for their crimes in World War Two. I always have to preface this by saying, of course, I come from a country that's just engaged in a war in Vietnam and killed millions of people and seems to have forgotten about it in about thirty days.

The extent to which they forgot about it was pretty remarkable. Just a couple of months ago, March 2002, was the fortieth anniversary of the public announcement that the United States is attacking South Vietnam, that U.S. pilots are bombing South Vietnam, that they began to use chemical warfare for crop destruction and started driving millions of people into concentration camps.

This is all in South Vietnam. No Russians, no Chinese, not any North Vietnamese, assuming they're not allowed to be in their own country. Just a U.S. war against South Vietnam, openly announced, and there is no commemoration after forty years because nobody even knows. It's not important. It's if they do something to us, the world is coming to an end. But if we do it to them, it's so normal, why should we even talk about it?

And likewise in Japan.

I think it's better in Japan. Japan was defeated, and defeated countries are forced to pay some attention to what they did. Victors never are. Take a look at the Tokyo trials. Undoubtedly the people were guilty of all kinds of crimes, but the trials were a total farce. From a legal or any other point of view, they were disgraceful. And did anybody try the U.S. criminals?

In fact, it's kind of interesting, in Nuremberg, the way the principles were constructed. They had to decide at Nuremberg what was going to count as a war crime. And there was a very explicit definition, and it was conscious. It was not hidden. A crime is a war crime if the Germans committed it and we didn't.

So, for example, bombing of urban concentrations was not a war crime because the British and the Americans did more of it than the Germans did, so therefore it's not a war crime. And German submarine commanders were able to bring testimony in defense by American submarine commanders who said, "Yeah, we did the same thing," and they were therefore freed because it wasn't a crime.

And it gets even worse than this. For example, opening the dikes in Holland was considered a war crime, properly. But in North Korea a few years later, after the U.S. Air Force had wiped out the whole country—there wasn't anything left to bomb—they started bombing the dams. That's a huge war crime. That's much worse than bombing the dikes. It was described, but it was described with pride.

If you read the official air force history or the *Air Force Quarterly* and so on, they describe it in gruesome detail, but about what a great achievement it was to bomb these dams, to see the huge flood of water scooping out valleys, and see the rage of the people. See, they are Asians who depend on rice. Here we're really getting them where it hurts. It's just like racist fanaticism, but praised. That's just a couple of years after they hanged German leaders who were doing much less than that.

And this is not part of history. Nobody knows. Unless you made a special study, you wouldn't know this.

Likewise in Vietnam, there were a lot of things...

I remember an article, which I wrote about at the time, in a leading U.S. journal, the *Christian Science Monitor*. It is a very good journal known for its piety, among other things, but in fact a very good journal. There was an article called "Trucks or Dams" by one of their main correspondents. And they raised the question, In Vietnam, should we bomb dams or should we bomb trucks?

And then it said, Well, bombing dams is much more satisfying because you see a big effect, and disaster, and lots of people starving, and so on. But despite the advantages, it still makes more sense tactically to bomb trucks because the trucks could be bringing in military equipment, and that could harm American soldiers, and so on. So, therefore, we should overcome our pleasure at bombing dams and instead bomb trucks. I don't even know how you comment on this. But what was striking about it was there was no reaction to it, absolutely no reaction.

Just to add another case, I think of all the things I've ever written, the one that probably aroused the most fury was a comment, something I said back about thirty-five years ago, when I said a question arises in the United States about whether what's needed is—I forget what term I used—dissent or denazification. And, boy, that really aroused fury. But it was about a particular incident. Here was the incident.

There was an item in the *New York Times* that described an event that took place in Chicago. The Chicago Museum of Science, which is a very respectable place, had put up an exhibit. The exhibit was a Vietnamese village, sort of a diorama of a Vietnamese village, and around it there were guns, and children were supposed to come and play, and shoot at the village with the guns. That was the game. And some women, a group of women protested. There was a small protest outside saying they didn't think that this was right. And the *New York Times* article was denouncing the protesters for daring to disrupt this wonderful event for children. And that's when I said, You sometimes wonder whether what's needed is dissent or denazification. And I think that's correct.

I mean, when you have the world's leading newspaper berating women for opposing this wonderful game where children shoot into a village, when it's actually going on. You know, it's like it would be bad enough if it was something from hundreds of years ago, but it's going on under your eyes. That's real striking. Again, not only no protests, but if anybody dares to protest, they're condemned.

Just to mention another incident, this one relevant to Japan. Back around the mid-1960s, the Rand Corporation, a big research agency connected with the Defense Department, translated and published Japanese counterinsurgency documents from Manchuria and North China. And I read them and I wrote an article in which I compared them to U.S. counterinsurgency documents in Vietnam. They were quite similar, the same self-righteousness, justifications, same procedures, and so on.

It wasn't a very popular article, but the only reference I've ever seen to it was in a scholarly article about Japanese atrocities in Manchuria and North China. It mentioned in a footnote that there was an interesting article that tried to justify these atrocities, namely mine. How was I justifying them? Well, I was comparing what the Japanese did to what the Americans were doing at the same time. And since what the Americans are doing must be right and just, by definition, that must have been a justification for the Japanese atrocities.

The author couldn't perceive that maybe it's the opposite. That's inconceivable because that would mean that maybe something we're doing is wrong.

You've been at this for many, many years, pointing out these kinds of discrepancies. Can you describe a little bit about how you became an activist?

Actually, those views go back to childhood. The first article I wrote, I know exactly when I wrote it because I remember the event. It was February 1939, after the fall of Barcelona. It was about the spread of fascism in Europe. I was ten years old. I wasn't an activist. But it's been a large part of my life ever since then.

There was a period of quiescence in the late 1950s when the whole country was quiet. But as soon as things began to heat up again in the early 1960s, I got back into it, with some regret and trepidation, I should say, because I know very well that you can't do these things part-time. If you get started, it's going to be all-consuming, and I had lots of things I was very happy doing and didn't want to give them up.

But you chose to?

Somehow.

Or felt you had to?

Well, by the time the beginnings of the Vietnam War were coming along, it was just impossible not to become involved.

And during those early years, what was the response to the work that you were doing?

Mostly it was total incomprehension. The Vietnam War actually began for the United States in 1950, and from 1954 to 1960, the United States had a kind of Latin American–style terror regime in place. And it wasn't any joke; they killed about sixty thousand to seventy thousand people. But there was no protest. Zero.

When Kennedy took over, they escalated it, and pretty soon it became a direct U.S. attack. Still no protest. Through the early 1960s, you couldn't get anybody to sign a petition. Nobody would come to a meeting. I remember it. We used to try to organize meetings on Vietnam, some of the students, a few others who were interested. But we would have to put together half a dozen topics—I mean, Iran, Venezuela, Vietnam, six other topics, and then maybe you'd get more people than organizers.

By 1965 or 1966, Vietnam was becoming a big issue. But protests were met with extreme hostility. Take Boston, right here. This is a pretty liberal city, but we couldn't have public protests against the war. They would be violently broken up. The speakers would be saved from being murdered only by hundreds of state police. And the attack on the protesters would be praised in the liberal media.

We had meetings in churches that were attacked. Arlington Street Church downtown was attacked, a meeting was attacked. Again, there were police to prevent them from breaking in and killing everybody. But that's about it. And the church was defaced, and everyone thought that that was right. It was considered the right thing to do.

I remember my wife—I had two little girls—my wife and the two kids went to a women's protest. You know what it's like, I mean, they're not throwing stones. Just people walking around with children. And this was in Concord. It's a suburb, a quiet, professional, upper middle class suburb. And they were attacked, people throwing tin cans and tomatoes and so on. It was considered right.

It wasn't until late 1966 that there was enough of a change for you to see substantial public opposition. That was five years after the war started. By then, there were hundreds of thousands of American troops rampaging around South Vietnam. And the war, of course, extended to the rest of Indochina. And nobody knows how many people were killed because nobody counted.

Another interesting thing about the Vietnam War is we have no idea what the costs were to the Vietnamese. I mean, for the United States, we know down to the last person. And the big postwar issue is finding the bones of American pilots. But nobody has any idea how many Vietnamese died or are still dying, for that matter. The guesses literally vary within millions. Because, who cares, you don't consider it when you slaughter other people.

Just a couple of weeks ago, there was a front-page story in all the papers. Some scientists have discovered that it would be possible to construct what are called "dirty bombs"—bombs that would have a lot of radiation but not much destructive impact—and to put them in New York somewhere. They calculated the effects and they said there wouldn't be many deaths, just a small number, but maybe a lot of disease, and it would certainly cause panic. So it's a horrible story, front-page news.

The same day, there was a conference in Hanoi, in which leading U.S. scientists participated, people who had worked on dioxin, the main poisonous ingredient in Agent Orange. The conference was concerned with the effects of U.S. chemical warfare on South Vietnam, only South Vietnam. The North was spared this terror. And an American scientist at the conference tested dioxin levels in various parts of the country.

Of course, those who had been subjected to crop

destruction and other uses of Agent Orange had very high levels, in fact hundreds of times as high as permissible in the United States. And these are also recent cases. Many of them are just from the last few years, children. And they tried to calculate the effects, which would be colossal, probably hundreds of thousands of victims. That news was hardly even mentioned in the press.

I had a friend do a database search. There were a couple of mentions here and there. So, here, a report on our use of chemical weapons, which may have killed maybe hundreds of thousands of people: not a mention. A report that maybe it *might* be possible to do something in New York that *might* kill a few people: front-page news.

That's the difference. That's the difference in who counts and who doesn't count.

How do you explain it? Journalists like to think of themselves as the champions of the people, investigative journalists revealing the way that things are really working, muckraking and so forth. And yet, things like that just don't get reported. How is that?

Partly it's just internalization of values. I mean, you don't consider that what you do to other people matters. It's not just journalists. It's true of scholarship, for example. It's true of the general intellectual world.

For example, if you take a poll among U.S. intellectuals, support for bombing Afghanistan is just overwhelming. But how many of them think that you should bomb Washington because of the U.S. war against Nicaragua, let's say, or Cuba or Turkey or anyone else? Now, if anyone were to suggest this, they would be considered insane. But why? I mean, if one is right, why is the other one wrong?

When you try to get someone to talk about this question, they can't comprehend what your question is. They can't comprehend that we should apply to ourselves the standards you apply to others. That is incomprehensible. There couldn't be a moral principle more elementary. All you have to do is read George Bush's favorite philosopher [Jesus]. There's a famous definition in the Gospels of the hypocrite, and the hypocrite is the person who refuses to apply to himself the standards he applies to others.

By that standard, the entire commentary and discussion of the so-called War on Terror is pure hypocrisy, virtually without exception. Can anybody understand that? No, they can't understand it.

And for those who would say, Wait a minute, let's think about this from a broader perspective, the bar is set higher for them, isn't it?

Not only is the bar higher, but if you try to do it, you're immediately denounced as an apologist for Osama bin Laden. I mean, the response is just total hysteria and irrationality. But that's not so unusual. I bet you anything, if you went back to Japan in the 1930s or 1940s, and you did a poll of intellectuals on the war, you would probably get the same reactions. I know it was true in Germany and France and everywhere else. It's just standard. It's ugly, but it's standard.

And now, coming back to the States—I live in Tokyo—coming back here and reading commentary about the coming war on Iraq, it's almost like they're writing it on a schedule.

It's a technical question. How much will it cost? Will there be problems?

In fact, Afghanistan is an interesting case. You can't take a poll in Afghanistan, but there was Afghan opinion expressed.

For example, the major women's group in Afghanistan, the Revolutionary Association of the Women of Afghanistan, which is highly regarded and very courageous; they have been fighting for women's rights for years. They have a Web site. They speak. They talk in words. They were strongly opposed to the bombing.

The United States organized a meeting in Pakistan in late October 2001 of one thousand Afghan leaders, some of whom trekked in from Afghanistan, others were in Pakistan. Those were all under U.S. auspices. They had disagreed about all sorts of things, but they were unanimous in opposing the bombing. Not only were they opposed in general, but they said it was harming their efforts to overthrow the Taliban from within, which they thought could succeed.

The same was true of the person that the United States had the most hope and faith for, Abdul Haq, a well-known Afghan dissident who was living in Pakistan. He was interviewed by the Carnegie Endowment for International Peace, not an obscure organization, and the interview was not published here but it was published in Europe. About that time, he condemned the bombing. He said the same thing. He said, It's harming our efforts to overthrow the Taliban, which we can do. And then he added that the Americans are doing this only because they want to show their muscle. They don't care anything about what happens to Afghanistan or Afghans. Just as they didn't care in the 1980s, they don't care now.

This is Afghan opinion. Did anybody pay any attention? Hardly a mention. Who cares what the Afghans think? We'll do what we want.

Turning our attention to Palestine and Israel, could the same thing be said for this thirty-five years of occupation that's been going on with hardly anybody even aware that it's an occupation?

In fact, it's not just an occupation. It's a very brutal occupation, like military occupations are. They're not pleasant. And this one was particularly harsh because the intent really was to demoralize and, if possible, remove the population. It couldn't go on without U.S. support, and the United States has been blocking any diplomatic settlement for about thirty years. The United States, of course, provides the military and economic support.

And when Israeli settlements spread over the region to sort of integrate the desired parts of the territories into Israel, it's the U.S. taxpayer. If fifty thousand people are tortured, which is the estimate, it's the U.S. taxpayer. Nothing counts. When they invaded Lebanon and killed twenty thousand people, the United States not only provided the means but vetoed Security Council resolutions to try to stop it, and so on. It didn't matter. None of this is an atrocity. The only atrocity is when they do something to Israel.

The only issue now is suicide bombers. And when did the suicide bombers begin? Last year, on a major scale. They're crimes, undoubtedly terrible crimes. One year of Palestinian crimes against Israel after thirty-four years of quiet. Israel had been nearly immune. I mean, there were terrorist attacks on Israel but not from within the occupied territories. The occupied territories were remarkably passive, and that's the way it's supposed to be. That's like Europe and its colonies. But when it goes the other way, it's a horrifying atrocity.

And in fact, the United States is escalating it right now. In December 2001, the Security Council tried to pass a European Union–initiated resolution calling for a dispatch of international monitors, just to reduce the level of violence, which has that effect. I mean, if there are international observers around, it tends to reduce violence. The United States vetoed it.

A week before that, there was a very important meeting in Geneva of the high-contracting parties for the Fourth Geneva Convention. I think 114 countries came, including the entire European Union, even Britain. And they reaffirmed what has been internationally affirmed over and over again, even with U.S. support, that the Fourth Convention applies to the occupied territories.

And then they went on to point out, which is correct, that that means virtually everything Israel is doing, meaning the United States and Israel are doing, is illegal, in fact, a war crime. And many of them they defined as "grave breaches," that is, serious war crimes. That means that the United States and Israeli leadership should be brought to trial. In fact, as a high-contracting party, the United States is obligated to prosecute people who carry out grave breaches of the Geneva Conventions, including its own leadership.

The United States didn't attend the meeting, which essentially kills it. It was barely reported here. That enhances atrocities. That means that grave breaches of the Geneva Convention, serious war crimes, the kind that people were tried for at Tokyo and Nuremberg, are legitimized. And they therefore continue. And you can go on and on, but the United States has unilaterally blocked any settlement of this, and still does.

There's a lot of talk now about the Saudi peace plan. Of course, the United States doesn't accept it, but it's a "wonderful step forward." Something like the Saudi peace plan has been on the table for twenty-five years. It was proposed at the Security Council in 1976. The United States vetoed it. Everybody in the world who mattered supported it, including the important Arab states and the PLO. And it's been going on like that ever since.

Do you know how many people in the academic world know about this? Probably ten. I mean, it's just hidden. The United States is carrying out something called a "peace process." A peace process, by definition, means whatever the United States is doing. For the last thirty years, the peace process has been the United States undermining peace. Does anybody know about this? No. I mean, if I talk about it to an educated audience, an academic audience, nobody will even know what I'm talking about. It can't be. How can the United States be undermining peace?

Why is it that the United States and Israel are often two against the rest of the world for United Nations resolutions?

The United States is usually one against the rest of the world because Israel doesn't vote in the Security Council. I mean, it's on all sorts of issues having nothing to do with the Middle East. So again, a standard belief in the West is that until Communism collapsed, the Russians were blocking action at the United Nations. That's the standard belief. In fact, when the Soviet Union collapsed, there was commentary in the *New York Times* about how at last the United Nations will be able to function without the Russian veto.

If you look at the record of vetoes, it's very illuminating. And the record of vetoes is just a plain, factual matter; there's nothing controversial about it. It's perfectly true that in the late 1940s and in the early 1950s, the Russians were vetoing a lot. And the reason was plain: the United States was so powerful that it could use the UN as an instrument of its own foreign policy. So of course the Russians were vetoing things.

By the 1950s, that began to change. Decolonization set in. The UN became more representative of the world. The other industrial countries revived. By the 1960s, the UN was not under control anymore. From the 1960s until today, the United States is far in the lead in vetoing resolutions. Britain is second, France is a distant third, and the Russians are fourth. It's exactly the opposite of the standard picture. And this is not true just on issues of the Middle East; it's on all kinds of issues.

The reason is very simple. The most powerful state in the world is not going to accept international authority. No other state would accept it, either, if it could get away with it. If Andorra could get away with it, they'd do what they want. But in the world as it exists, the only people that can do what they want are the more powerful.

It seems as if the United States is ignoring European opinion.

It always has.

Even more now?

It ignores its own opinion. I mean, take the Middle East again. The majority of the U.S. population, a considerable majority, supports the Saudi plan. The United States opposes it. If you tell people, Look, it's your own government that's blocking what you support, they won't know what you're talking about, because nobody knows that. To know that requires a research project.

So, yes, it's domestic opinion, too, that is ignored. And it's not just now, but it's always. And it's not just the United States, it's anybody else who can get away with it.

Will that ever change?

It's changed. It's better than it was thirty or forty years ago. For example, now the U.S. government is subjected to human rights requirements imposed by Congress on arms shipments and so on. They usually find a way to evade it, but nevertheless, the constraints are there. Why are they there? That's a result of the 1960s again.

The population of the country is a lot more civilized than it was forty years ago, and this increases. And that imposes constraints on state violence. There's no other way. I mean, there's no external force that can constrain the violence of the most powerful state, whether it's the United States or anyone else. But the constraints can come from within.

When you were in Palo Alto, you spoke about the militarization of space and pointed out the discrepancies between the most powerful country in the world and the other countries of the world. And that discrepancy and that gap are getting larger and larger. Will that have a fundamental impact on the way things play out?

It's already having it. In fact, the current U.S. leadership is extreme in this respect. But they are quite frankly and openly committed to the use of violence to control the world, and they say so.

So, for example, when Prince Abdullah of Saudi Arabia was here a couple of weeks ago, he tried to persuade U.S. leaders to moderate their support for Israeli violence. And what Abdullah said is there's going to be an uprising in the Arab world that will be very dangerous for your own interests, like control of oil. Their reaction was interesting. He was dismissed, of course.

But on interesting grounds, he was told—it was reported in the *New York Times*, you can read it—what they said is, Look, just take a look at what we did to Iraq during

Desert Storm. Now we're ten times that strong. If you want to see how strong, take a look at what we just did in Afghanistan. That's what it's for, to show you what can happen to you if you raise your head. So if you don't do what we tell you, you'll just be pulverized. We don't care what you think or what you say.

That's their attitude. And they say so, and it's evident in the actions. That's not very good for the world, or for the people in the United States.

It seems that in some ways, we can't mount a war like the war in Vietnam anymore, a sustained war like that.

Because there's no popular support for it.

But on the other hand, the demonization of people like Saddam Hussein and the Taliban gives the government free reign.

That's a choice of the intellectual classes. Take Saddam Hussein. Every time Blair or Bush or Clinton or Madeleine Albright or someone calls for a war on Iraq, they always say it the same way. They say, This is the worst monster in history. How can we allow him to exist? He even committed the ultimate crime: he used gas "against his own people." How can such a person exist?

All of which is correct, except for what's missing. He did use gas against "his own people" (actually, Kurds are hardly his own people), *with our support.* He carried out the Anfal operation, maybe killing one hundred thousand Kurds, with our support. He was developing weapons of mass destruction at a time when he was really dangerous, and we provided him the aid and support to do it, perfectly consciously. He was a friend and ally, and he remained so.

Try to find someone who's added those words in any of the commentary. He's a monster, but he did it with our support because we didn't care. Almost nobody wrote that. So, yes, they can demonize Saddam Hussein but must exclude the fact that his worst crimes by far were committed with U.S. and British support. And that's not just demonizing him, it's very selective demonization.

The most you'll find sometimes is that we didn't pay enough attention to his crimes. It's not that we didn't pay attention. We didn't care. The leadership didn't care. He was performing a valuable service, no matter how awful he was. In fact, Iraq is the only country outside of Israel that was given dispensation to attack an American ship, a U.S. Navy vessel, and kill about thirty-five sailors. Most countries can't get away with that. Israel got away with it in 1967, and Iraq got away with it in 1988.

Iraqi missiles hit a U.S. destroyer in the Gulf, killing, I think, thirty-seven sailors. We didn't care. Iraq is a friend and ally. Hussein's our man, so it was a mistake. Nobody else could get away with that. They have to be very high on the list of friends to be given that privilege. And that was at the peak of his atrocities.

Just quickly, in terms of that kind of alliance, Japan's involvement in Indonesia and the East Timor issue. Japan has provided a great deal of overseas development aid.

More than that. I saw some of it firsthand. I never talked about this, but if you'd like to know, I was testifying at the UN on East Timor in 1978, I guess. There were church groups and others who induced the UN to allow some critical testimony.

I remember sitting there one entire day at the UN building, waiting to be called on to testify, and it wasn't coming up because of bureaucratic maneuverings in the background to try to block the testimony. I thought at first it was from the United States, but it wasn't. It was from Japan. Japan was so protective of Indonesia that they didn't want to permit testimony at the UN that would criticize the Indonesian invasion, and that was at the peak of the atrocities.

They weren't alone. In fact, the whole world has a horrible record on this. I mean, it's all suppressed now. But right at the peak of the atrocities, the United States was providing most of the arms. Britain came in during 1978. That's the Labor government, not Thatcher. Nineteen seventy-eight was when the atrocities peaked. That's when the total of East Timorese killed was running up to two hundred thousand. Britain saw a great opportunity to send arms. They became the main arms supplier and remained so right through to 1999. France joined in; a couple of years later, Sweden joined in; Holland. Anybody who could make some money or get some privileges by slaughtering East Timorese was pretty happy to do it. Now they're all applauding the new nation that we brought into being with our generosity and so on. All of this is gone. It's not ancient history, but it's gone.

The question that often comes to people's minds is the connection between your work in linguistics and your political work.

There's really no direct connection. I could just as well be an algebraic topologist and do the same things. There's a more remote connection, possibly. People are interested in linguistics for all sorts of reasons, but my own interest since the beginning, for fifty years, has been as a way of exploring some aspects of human higher mental faculties, and ultimately of human nature, which should show up in every domain. Language happens to be one of the few areas where you can study very core human capacities, unique and core human capacities, in a very intense way and achieve some results that go beyond superficial understanding. In most areas, it's very hard to do it, but this is one area in which you can.

At the core of this capacity for language, it's been recognized for centuries, is what is sometimes called a creative aspect, the free ability to do what you and I are doing—to express our own thoughts without limit, within constraints but without limit, in novel ways, and so on. This ability is somehow a fundamental part of human nature. It's the core of Cartesian philosophy, for example. And you can learn something, not about how we do it, that's beyond inquiry, but at least about the mechanisms that enter into it.

Well, similar questions arise in every aspect of human capacity, and again, it's traditional. David Hume, two hundred and fifty years ago, pointed out that the foundation of morals must be what we nowadays call generative gram-

mar. He didn't call it that, but it must be some set of principles that we're capable of applying in novel situations—
again, without limit. And he pointed out that these principles have to be part of our nature, because there's no way
to acquire them from experience. He didn't go on to point
it out, but it also follows that they must be uniform. In
fact, he wouldn't have said that, because they didn't think
that humans were uniform at that time, but now we know
that humans are almost interchangeable. There's very little genetic variation in the species, minuscule. We probably all derived from a small breeding group not very long
ago, so we're basically the same creature, which means
that these principles have to be uniform as well.

Also, in theory, you can learn something about these
aspects of human nature, moving over to the domain of
human affairs, including politics, but also personal life or
anything else. Anyone who takes any stand on anything—
say you're in favor of keeping things the way they are, or
some minor reform, or revolution, or whatever it may be.
If you're serious about it, if you're acting as a kind of
moral agent and you think what you do should meet certain minimum moral standards, you're taking that position because you think it's good for people. It's going to
somehow bring out and amplify and offer possibilities for
their fundamental nature to express itself.

Well, at that point, there's a theoretical connection, but
it's pretty abstract, because when you deal with anything
as complex as human beings, you're always on the surface.
In fact, we can't answer questions like this about insects.
It will be a long time, if ever, before one can have anything

like scientific understanding of any questions like these. So there's a kind of connection in spirit, but no deductive connections.

But there's a sense in which your appeal to first principles in political and moral affairs...

It's similar. It's a kind of family resemblance. But we don't know anywhere near enough to think of drawing close connections.

NOTE

1. In March 1995, members of the Japanese group Aum Shinrikyo attacked a Tokyo subway by releasing the poison gas sarin, killing twelve people and injuring thousands.

PART II

U.S. *Arms, Human Rights, and Social Health*

A talk sponsored by the Albert Einstein College of Medicine Muslim Students' Association and others, at the Montefiore Medical Center, Bronx, New York, May 25, 2002, followed by an excerpt from a question-and-answer session with the audience.

WHAT I'D LIKE TO CONSIDER WITH YOU TODAY is the U.S. role in the world—what it is today, what it is likely to be tomorrow. The reasons for concentrating on the United States should be too obvious to mention, but I'll mention them. The most obvious reason is that the United States is the most important power in the world. It has overwhelming military force and other forms of power. It has a determinative impact on anything that happens in contemporary world history.

The second reason is, of course, that we're here. We happen to have an unusual degree of freedom in the United States, and, for most of us, privilege. That confers enormous responsibility for our own actions, and for our influence on policy. Even if it were not the case that this is by far the most powerful country in the world, that responsibility would or should be of primary concern to us.

I apologize for even mentioning this. It's an obvious truism that shouldn't have to be mentioned, and I do so only because when anyone tries to pursue this transparently obvious course, which follows the most elementary political and moral truisms, it elicits the most intriguing reactions. I won't talk about that, but it's worth thinking about.

One way to measure the U.S. role in the world—there are many—is by looking at U.S. aid, in particular, military aid. It's not a very attractive topic because, as is well known, U.S. foreign aid is the most miserly by far of any of the major industrial countries. And if we take away the component that goes to one rich country and another middle-range country (because of its association with the rich country), namely Israel and Egypt, there's almost nothing left. However, if you count everything, it's still grotesquely marginal, and it is declining.

But there is, nevertheless, some aid, and quite a lot of military aid, in fact. And that's worth looking at, because it gives some kind of an indication of what the United States is doing in the world; not the only indication, but a good one. The connection between U.S. aid and foreign policy has indeed been the subject of some academic work.

One well-known study, by the leading academic specialist on human rights in Latin America, Lars Schoultz, of the University of North Carolina, looked at U.S. aid in Latin America. He wrote an article about twenty years ago, in which he pointed out that there is a very close correlation between U.S. aid and human rights abuses in Latin America. To quote him, "U.S. aid flows disproportionately to Latin American governments which torture their citizens...to the hemisphere's relatively egregious violators of fundamental human rights." That was twenty years ago.

About the same time, Edward Herman, a coauthor of mine and an economist at the Wharton School at the University of Pennsylvania, did a worldwide study looking at the same question, specifically at the relation between U.S. aid and torture. It turned out there was a surprisingly, unpleasantly high correlation between U.S. foreign aid and torture. Take a look at the Amnesty International records on torture and U.S. foreign aid and the connection is very close.

Statistical correlations obviously don't tell you about causal relations. And it's unlikely that the U.S. government has any specific interest in torture. Therefore, he did another study, a much more important one. He studied the correlation between U.S. aid and other factors, and it turned out that one of the best correlations was between U.S. aid and improvement in the investment climate. So, as a country improves opportunities for investors to extract resources and so on, foreign aid goes up.

Well, that's a very natural correlation. That makes perfect sense. That's what you would expect U.S. policy to be directed toward, and it is. And the fact that aid is correlated with improvement in the investment climate is not surprising.

Well, how do you improve the investment climate in a third-world country? One of the best ways is to murder union organizers and peasant leaders, to torture priests, to massacre peasants, to undermine social programs, and so on. That does have a way of improving the investment climate. And that yields a secondary correlation, the kind that Lars Schoultz discovered, namely between U.S. foreign aid and egregious human rights violations.

And that's probably the explanation. It's not that the United States has any particular interest in egregious human rights violations. It's just that it's a natural corollary to what it is interested in, and to how you achieve goals like that.

Well, that was twenty years ago. About the time that these studies came out, the Reagan administration came into office, as you'll recall. The Reagan administration came into office announcing very loud and clear that the focus of U.S. foreign policy would be a "War on Terror." And they focused particularly on what was called, in the words of Secretary of State George Shultz, "the evil scourge of terrorism," a plague spread by "depraved opponents of civilization itself" in "a return to barbarism in the modern age."

Shultz, who was considered a moderate within the Reagan administration, went on to say that terrorism had to be dealt with by force and violence, not by utopian legalistic means like mediation and negotiations and so on, which were just a sign of weakness. The Reagan administration declared that the fight would be focused on the two areas where this crime was most severe, namely Central America and the Middle East.

Now let's turn to the outcomes. What happened in Central America and the Middle East? Keep in mind that we're still asking about the correlation between U.S. aid and other aspects of policy. Incidentally, I should mention that Lars Schoultz's study pointed out that the correlation between egregious human rights violations and aid held specifically for military aid. The aid was independent of need, and he checked on that. And it ran right through the period of the Carter administration, up to 1980. It continued despite the human rights rhetoric.

So, what happened in Central America and the Middle East in the 1980s in fighting the "War on Terror"? Central America was turned into a graveyard. Hundreds of thousands of people were massacred—two hundred thousand, approximately—over a million refugees, orphans, great masses of torture, every conceivable form of barbarism.

With one country, Nicaragua, the United States had to basically attack it, because it didn't have an army to carry out the terror as it did in the other countries. The U.S. attack against Nicaragua was quite serious. It led to tens of thousands of people killed, and the country virtually destroyed. It's now the second poorest country in the hemisphere, and it may never recover.

Because, in this case, the United States was attacking a country, not just the people of the country (as in El Salvador, Guatemala, and Honduras), the country was able to follow means of recourse that are available to states. It responded in the way that a law-abiding state is supposed to respond to massive international terrorism: it went to the international institutions. First Nicaragua went to the World Court, which condemned the United States for international terrorism, for "unlawful use of force," and for violation of treaties. It ordered the U.S. government to terminate the crimes and to pay massive reparations.

The United States responded by instantly escalating the war (with bipartisan support, incidentally) and, for the first time, giving official orders to attack what are called "soft targets"—health clinics, agricultural cooperatives, and so on. This went on until finally the population voted for the U.S. candidate and the terror stopped in 1990.

After the United States rejected the World Court judgment, Nicaragua went to the UN Security Council. The United States would have been condemned by the Security Council, but the United States, of course, vetoed the resolution, which called on all states to observe international law. So, the current leader of the "War on Terror" is the only state in the world that's been condemned by the World Court for international terrorism and that has vetoed a resolution calling on all states to observe international law, a fact that perhaps is relevant to the current situation. You'll search very hard to find any mention in the press of anything I'm talking about, which has to do with the first phase of the "War on Terror," and which is obviously not irrelevant.

What about the other countries of Central America? Well, they fared far worse than Nicaragua. In Nicaragua, the people had an army to defend them. In the other countries, the terrorist force attacking the population *was* the army. In El Salvador and Guatemala, it was even worse than Nicaragua in this period.

Actually, El Salvador became the leading recipient of U.S. military aid during this period (putting aside Israel and Egypt, a separate category). It was carrying out some of the worst atrocities. And the "counterterrorist war" was a success. If you want to find out what a success it was, just take a look at the documents produced by the notorious School of the Americas. One of their slogans—their talking points, as they put it—is (I'm quoting) the U.S. army "helped to defeat liberation theology." That's pretty accurate. One of the main targets of the U.S. "War on Terror" was the Catholic Church, which had made the grave error of turning toward what they called "the preferential option for the poor" and had to be punished for that.

El Salvador is a dramatic example. The decade of the 1980s opened with the murder of an archbishop. It ended with the murder of six leading Jesuit intellectuals. And the U.S. army defeated liberation theology.

An interesting fact about our intellectual culture is that nobody knows anything about this. If six leading Czech intellectuals and an archbishop had been murdered by Russian-backed, Russian-armed and -trained forces, we'd know about it. We'd know their names and we'd have read their books. But you might do a little experiment and find out how many people you know, educated people, can even tell you the names of the Jesuit intellectuals—the leading Latin American intellectuals who were murdered by the elite forces that we armed and trained—or the archbishop, or of any of the seventy thousand others, most of whom were peasants, as usual.

You know the answers without checking, and they tell us something interesting about ourselves, something that is worth knowing.

Well, that's the success of the "War on Terror" in Central America, the first focus.

Now what about the Middle East, the second focus of

the "War on Terror"? Well, it's true, there were plenty of state-sponsored terrorist atrocities in the Middle East at that time. The worst of them by a huge margin was the Israeli invasion of Lebanon in 1982; it ended up killing about twenty thousand people.

This was international terrorism. It was able to proceed because the United States gave the green light, provided the arms, and provided the diplomatic support—vetoing several UN Security Council resolutions that tried to get the fighting stopped and the forces to retreat. And it was a grand success as well. The chief of staff of the Israeli army, Lt. Gen. Rafael Eitan, pointed out right away that the operation had been a success. It removed the Palestinian Liberation Organization (PLO) as a factor in negotiations for the occupied territories.

Indeed, that was the goal of the war; it had nothing to do with Lebanon. In fact, in Israel it was openly called "a war for the occupied territories." The PLO was getting extremely annoying with its insistence on negotiated settlement of the conflict. Israel didn't want that, and they succeeded in destroying the PLO, driving it out of the region, which was a grand success.

That's a textbook illustration of international terrorism. If you take the official U.S. government definition of terrorism—the threat or use of violence to achieve political, religious, or other ends through intimidation, inducing fear, and so on, directed against civilian populations—Israel's invasion of Lebanon is a textbook example. You couldn't have a clearer example. International terrorism, because of the decisive U.S. role.

Notice, incidentally, that I'm giving the United States the benefit of the doubt. You might argue that this is much worse than international terrorism, that it's outright aggression. In fact, that's what you should call it. If it's outright aggression, then it calls for Nuremberg trials for the U.S. leadership and the Israeli leadership. But giving them the benefit of the doubt, we'll call it only international terrorism. And it's a clear case, by far the worst case of that decade.

Incidentally, there's been twenty years of lying in the United States about the reasons for the war. But you have to give credit where credit is due. The *New York Times* finally came clean on January 24, 2002. If you read it carefully, there's a sentence buried in a report on another topic by James Bennet, which tells the truth.

For the first time I've ever seen it in the United States, he describes what was well known in Israel twenty years ago and what you could have read in the dissident literature for the last twenty years based on Israeli sources: that the war was fought for political reasons only. It was a war for the West Bank. The idea was to eliminate the threat of negotiations that was coming from the Palestinians.

That's true. It's been well known for twenty years to everybody except the American population. Now there's a sentence that tells the truth, so you can now quote the *New York Times* on this. This makes it official. The documentation on this is just overwhelming, from the first days of the invasion. So that's an improvement. If you wait long enough, good things happen.

Well, that's the worst act of terror in the Middle East.

There were others. The peak year for Middle East terrorism was 1985. It was in 1985 that the annual poll of newspaper editors by the Associated Press picked terrorism in the Middle East as the top story of the year. And in scholarship on terrorism as well, it's also picked as the top year. That makes sense. There was plenty of terrorism in 1985—not as bad as 1982, but bad enough.

What were the worst terrorist acts in the Middle East in the peak year, 1985? There are three candidates for first prize. Nothing else even comes close. One candidate is a car bomb in Beirut, which was placed outside a mosque and timed to go off when people were leaving the mosque, so as to kill the maximum number of people. It did. It killed eighty people and wounded 250 others. It was a powerful bomb that killed babies in their beds down the street.

Most of those killed were women and girls leaving the mosque. The bomb was aimed at a Muslim sheik, who escaped. It was traced back to the CIA and British intelligence, and that's not particularly contested. That's one candidate for the prize of worst terrorist act in the Middle East in the peak year of 1985.

The second candidate would be the Israeli bombing of Tunis a couple of months later. Tunis was attacked with smart bombs. People were torn to pieces, and so on, and the attack killed about seventy-five people, Tunisians and Palestinians. They were civilians. It was pretty graphically described by a top Israeli reporter in the Hebrew-language press in Israel, but there was not very much reporting here. This was, again, international terrorism. The

United States was deeply involved. For one thing, the Sixth Fleet, which is in the area, did not inform the Tunisians—Tunisia is an ally—that the bombers were on their way, although of course they knew it.

Secretary of State George Shultz responded to the bombing by immediately calling the Israeli foreign minister, congratulating Israel, and expressing U.S. sympathy for the terrorist assault. Actually, Shultz drew back from this open praise for the massacre when the UN Security Council passed a resolution unanimously condemning Israel for an act of armed aggression. The United States abstained on that vote and kind of backed off.

But again, giving the benefit of the doubt to the United States and Israel, let's just call this international terrorism instead of, like the rest of the world, an act of armed aggression. That's a second candidate. There was no pretense that this was in defense, just like there wasn't any in the Lebanon war.

The only other candidate I can think of is Shimon Peres's Iron Fist Operation in March 1985 in southern Lebanon. The Israeli army attacked what the high command called "terrorist villagers," and there were big massacres and atrocities. Lots of people were killed by the Israeli army or by its mercenary forces in the south. A lot of people were kidnapped and taken to Israel for interrogation, which means torture and imprisonment.

Nobody knows the scale, because there's a principle of journalism and scholarship that you don't investigate your own atrocities. We know down to the last person how many people were killed in some atrocity that you can attribute to someone else. But when we look at our own atrocities, we haven't even a clue.

For example, if you take the U.S. war in Vietnam, there were obviously millions of people killed, but the numbers aren't known within millions. Who would care to count? Or who would care to count how many hundreds of thousands of people have died from the effects of U.S. chemical warfare in South Vietnam? Outside of the United States, there have been some attempts to estimate, but here it's just not an issue. We don't care about things like that. And so it goes.

Therefore, we don't really know how many people were killed by U.S.-Israeli international terrorism in southern Lebanon or in the Iron Fist Operation. These attacks were carried out by the left-wing "peace party," which was in office at the time.

These are the only three examples that I know, and they're probably all about in the same range. There is no other act of international terrorism in the region that even comes close. So that's a good sample of the way the "War on Terror" was fought in the second major area, the Middle East.

Of course, it was fought elsewhere as well. For example, in southern Africa, where the estimates are that about a million and a half people were killed by South African depredations in the countries surrounding South Africa (forget what was happening inside South Africa). In Mozambique and Angola, about a million and a half people were killed and over sixty billion dollars of damage were caused, just in the Reagan years alone, 1980 to 1988.

Those are the years of what was called "constructive

engagement," at a time when South Africa was a valued ally and Nelson Mandela's African National Congress was identified as one of the "more notorious terrorist groups" in the world. That was in 1988, when South Africa was still, of course, a valued ally after its actions in the preceding eight years. (Again, I'm putting aside what happened inside South Africa.) And we can continue around the world.

Without proceeding, there are a number of conclusions that follow. One is that the correlation between U.S. aid and extraordinary human rights abuses became so close that it isn't even worth studying. In the 1960s and 1970s, you can study it, but in the 1980s, it's close to a one-to-one correlation.

I'm not even talking about social health, because it's redundant. When you do this to people, you don't have to talk about the health consequences. A second important conclusion has to do with continuity. Not only is this continuous with what happened before, but if you take a look at the people who are leading the current "War on Terror," what were they doing then?

Well, the military component of the current "War on Terror" is led by Donald Rumsfeld, who was Reagan's special envoy to the Middle East, sharing responsibility for the "War on Terror" that I've been describing. The diplomatic side of the current "War on Terror" is led by John Negroponte, appointed to the UN as ambassador to lead the "War on Terror." In those years, he was U.S. ambassador to Honduras, which was the base for U.S. terrorist operations in the region, specifically for preparing and supervising the war against Nicaragua.

So those are two leading figures in the current "War on Terror," and they played a very significant role in the first "War on Terror"; nor are they the only ones, which suggests something. Same people, same institutions, same policies. You expect the same outcomes, if you want to think about what the second phase of the current "War on Terror" will be like.

This is discussed in scholarship. To take one specific example, look at the December 2002 issue of *Current History*—a serious scholarly journal—which is devoted to terror and the problems of terror. The authors, who are noted scholars and analysts, identify the 1980s as the decade of state terror, which is correct. It was the decade of state terror.

And they describe the United States as having effectively combated state terror in that period by taking what are called "proactive measures." So the actions that I just described are proactive measures in defense against terror. They also suggest that the war against Nicaragua, for which the United States was condemned at the World Court, is a good model for future acts against terror. Specifically, two authors point out that the "contra" war against Nicaragua is a good model for the U.S. support for the Northern Alliance in Afghanistan.

The year 1985 in the Middle East is also mentioned. It's identified as the peak period of terror. And a couple of examples are given, but not the ones I mentioned, of course. They can't be mentioned. The examples that are mentioned as illustrating why 1985 was the peak period of terror are two incidents, in each of which one person was killed, an

American. One is a hijacking in which one American military officer was killed. Another is the *Achille Lauro*, the most famous incident, in which one person, Leon Klinghoffer, a crippled American, was murdered.

These are indeed acts of terror. One person was killed in each case. They're nothing like the acts that I described earlier, of course, but they are acts of terror. The killing of Leon Klinghoffer, which is very famous, is comparable, for example, to an incident that just took place in Jenin a couple of weeks ago, when a man in a wheelchair was trying to get out of the way of an Israeli tank and was crushed by the tank and his body torn to shreds. Or one that took place two days ago, when a young woman who was trying to get to a hospital for a dialysis treatment was blocked, prevented from getting there; she was also in a wheelchair, and she died. And there are other incidents that are comparable to this. It's easy to go on, just to show continuities. But of course, none of this counts as terror.

The *Achille Lauro* incident surely was terror. And it cannot be justified by the fact that it was undertaken in retaliation against the far worse terror of the Tunis attack a week earlier. You can't justify terror in retaliation. But of course, that observation generalizes. I'll leave it to you to draw the conclusions. That's assuming that we accept elementary moral principles, of course, and that we separate ourselves from one hundred percent of the discussion of this topic. Then the consequences follow.

That's not the end of the interpretation. If you read the same issue, you'll find that the leading academic specialist on terror, a professor at UCLA, traces the roots of Osama bin Laden much deeper, and not just to Islam. He traces it back to the Vietnam War and says that "Viet Cong terror against the American Goliath...kindled hopes that the Western heartland was vulnerable too." So, the American heartland was vulnerable in South Vietnam, when South Vietnamese were carrying out terror there against us.

Another exercise for the reader would be to explore, for example, the Nazi archives, and to see if you can find an analog to this analysis. You might try. It elicits no comment here, another interesting reflection on the nature of the moral and intellectual culture in which we live. This is something we ought to be concerned about, I think.

Let's go on. The acts of terror that I actually described in Central America, the Middle East, South Africa, and so forth, they don't count as terror. They do not enter into the annals of terror in the scholarly literature. They do enter, but not as terror. They enter as "counterterror" or as a "just war." And the principle is that if somebody carries out terror against us or against our allies, it's terror, but if we carry out terror or our allies do, maybe much worse terror, against someone else, it's not terror, it's counterterror or it's a just war.

Now that principle is, as far as I know, close to universal. You might explore the massive literature on the topic and see if you can find an exception to it. And it's not just the United States. As far as I know, it's universal. Anyplace I've looked—and I've looked in a lot of different countries— that's exactly what you find. During the whole history of European imperialism, this is the standard line: We do it to them, it's counterterror or a just war, bringing civilization to the barbarians, or something like that. If we do that in their own countries—because remember, until September 11, the West was largely immune—at a vastly worse level, it's not terror. It's a civilizing mission or something like that.

It was true with even the worst killers in history. They used the same techniques. Take, say, the Nazis. If you read the Nazi literature, in occupied Europe, they claimed to be defending the population and the legitimate governments against the terror of the partisans, who were directed from abroad. And like all propaganda, even the most vulgar, there's a thread of truth to that.

The partisans did carry out terror and there's no question that they were directed from London, so they were carrying out terror directed from abroad. And the Vichy government is about as legitimate as most of the governments that the United States installs throughout the world or that other imperial powers have, so there's some marginal justification for this grotesque Nazi propaganda, which has a close resemblance to ours.

The same is true of the Japanese in Manchuria and North China. They were bringing the people an earthly paradise, defending the nationalist government of Manchuria against the Chinese bandits, and so on. Very much like us.

Anyway, as far as I know, this is kind of a universal principle. We do it; it's counterterror, a just war, and so on. They do it; it's terror. Scale doesn't matter. Nothing matters.

Well, that's through the 1980s. Let's go on to the 1990s and the present, and see what's happened since. So let's take today, looking just at military aid, let's say. Put aside the top two, Israel and Egypt—they're in a separate category. Putting them aside, first place worldwide was El Salvador during the period of its government's massive terror campaign against the Salvadoran people. But after the U.S. army successfully defeated liberation theology, El Salvador dropped down, and first place was taken by Turkey. Turkey maintained first place until 1999, when it was replaced by Colombia.

On a personal note, I've just returned from two of these countries, from the sites of some of the worst terrorist atrocities in the 1990s, in southern Colombia last week and in southeastern Turkey a couple of weeks earlier.

Why Turkey? Turkey, of course, has always been a major recipient of U.S. military aid. It's strategically located, close to the Soviet Union, the Middle East, and so on. So it received a stable and high level of U.S. military aid right through the Cold War period. In 1984, that changed. Military aid shot up. In the Clinton years alone, U.S. military aid to Turkey was four times higher than in the entire Cold War period up until 1984. And in the year 1997, which was the peak year, it was higher than in the entire Cold War period up to 1984. That was serious aid. It provided eighty percent of the arms for Turkish armed forces, and it wasn't pistols: it was jet planes and tanks and military advisors and so on. What was the point? The reason was that during those years, peaking in the 1990s under Clinton, the Turkish government was carrying out state terror, mainly against the Kurds—approximately a quarter of the population. At that time, a major war was being carried out against them. That's the area I visited.

I'm borrowing the term "state terror" from several

sources. One is a well-known Turkish sociologist, Ismail Besikci, who wrote a book in 1991 called *State Terror in the Middle East,* including Turkish terror in the Kurdish areas. He was immediately imprisoned. As far as I know, he's still in prison. He had already served fifteen years in prison for reporting the facts on the Turkish repression of the Kurds, who have been miserably repressed for decades.

Besikci was offered a ten-thousand-dollar prize from the U.S. Fund for Freedom of Expression, but he turned it down because of the decisive U.S. support for state terror in Turkey. He couldn't accept an award from the United States while it was participating in Turkish state terrorism. His imprisonment the second time was protested very strongly by writers, scholars, and parliamentarians in Britain, but not in the United States, and the reason is because it's not terror, since we're doing it. Therefore what he's describing can't be terror, and we don't have to protest it.

Again, this is major U.S. participation in international terrorism. He's not the only one who used the term. In 1994, the Turkish state minister for human rights described the terror that his government was carrying out as state terror. At that time, he notes, two million people had been driven out of their homes; every imaginable kind of barbaric atrocity had been committed, with tens of thousands killed.

By now, it's much worse. When I was there recently, the highly respected head of the Kurdish human rights commission, Osman Baydemir (who, incidentally, is highly respected by the U.S. embassy as well), estimated that by now the toll is three million refugees, and fifty thousand killed. Many of the refugees, as I saw, live in caves outside the walls of the city of Diyarbakir, where I was, and other similar places.

Shortly after I was there, Osman Baydemir was picked up by the state security courts and indicted; he had committed a crime. Namely, there's a New Year's festival celebrated throughout the region and he had written about it, but in writing about it, he had used the Kurdish spelling rather than the Turkish spelling. They differ in that one has a *W* and one has a *V*. So he's now under indictment, with what consequences, we don't know.[1]

If a couple of children are wearing clothes that, when you put them together, turn out to be the Kurdish colors, that can be a serious threat and a crime. While I was there, a journalist was arrested and then jailed for playing a Kurdish song over the radio. His radio station was closed down. I was actually there for a political trial. A publisher was on trial for having published a collection of essays of mine that included about three sentences, drawn from standard human rights reports, on Turkish repression of the Kurds. There was enough international attention in that case so that the publisher was released. But he's on trial for six other similar crimes now. And so it continues.

While I was in Diyarbakir, a remarkable act of courage took place at the end of the talk, before a big audience and in front of television cameras and plenty of police cameras. Three students came up and presented me with a Kurdish-English dictionary, which is an act of enormous bravery. You can't describe it; you have to know the situation to know what that means. Nobody could figure out how the dictionary was sneaked into Turkey. I don't know what's happened to the students; it's hard to trace.

The students and others who protest the harsh laws and practices get plenty of support, incidentally. Istanbul is not like the United States. There are plenty of writers, journalists, and academics who constantly struggle against these Draconian laws and repression, and they face serious threats. They go to jail; it's not much fun to be in a Turkish jail. They're constantly doing it.

While I was there, they presented to the state prosecutor a copublished book of banned writings, including writings of people in jail, and demanded to be prosecuted. Again, because of the focus of international attention, it didn't happen. Those are the kinds of things that people do when they're really under repression, not like here, where privileged people pretend to be under repression. But these are the kinds of things that intellectuals do in places where they take civil rights and human rights seriously. They desperately need support of every kind, and primarily from here.

Well, there is a reaction here to Turkish state terror: it's highly praised. So for example, the State Department in 2000—after the terror campaign succeeded, if you like—published its annual report on terror and singled out Turkey for what it called its "positive experiences" in combating terror. It picked out Turkey, alongside of Algeria and Spain. I don't have to mention Algeria. In the case of Spain, I suppose they're referring to the Spanish officials who weren't yet in jail for counterterrorist atrocities. So these were the three countries picked out for their positive experiences in combating terror.

The U.S. ambassador to Turkey has just written in an academic journal that the United States could have no better friend and ally than Turkey, as demonstrated in its antiterror campaign, namely the one I've just described. And the Turkish government is quite grateful for this. The prime minister was the first to offer the United States ground troops for the "War against Terror" in Afghanistan, and he explained why. This was in gratitude for the U.S. assistance in helping the Turkish state combat terror in the manner to which I have just alluded.

The Turkish army is now protecting Kabul against terror with U.S. funding. This means that the troops that carried out some of the worst terrorist atrocities of the 1990s are now taking part in the "War against Terror," in both cases funded by the United States, itself a leading terrorist state, as is surely uncontroversial. And this elicits no comment. None. You can check and see. That again tells us something about ourselves. It's not that it's overlooked. I don't know what Orwell would have made of this, but we can make of it what we like.

In 1999, Colombia replaced Turkey as the leading recipient of U.S. arms. The reason was that Turkish atrocities had succeeded in repressing the population sufficiently. Colombian atrocities had not yet succeeded. And they are significant.

In the 1990s, Colombia had by far the worst human rights record in the hemisphere, and conforming to the standard correlations, it received more U.S. aid, including military aid, than the rest of the hemisphere combined. That's the normal relationship. The correlation continues.

The atrocities are horrifying. There's one that the Colombian state actually investigated, a chain saw massacre. The Colombian army went into an area and cut people up with chain saws and threw them in pits and so on. There was actually a punishment for that. The officer in charge was removed from his command, so you can't say there's impunity.

Colombia now has the world record in killing trade unionists and journalists. I was there a couple of years ago on an Amnesty International mission, part of a campaign to protect human rights defenders in various countries. They picked Colombia as the first place to go because it had by far the worst record in killing human rights defenders and advocates.

By now, apparently, political murders have risen to about ten to twenty a day. There are ten thousand new displaced people every month. That's added to the two million that were already displaced. They are driven into miserable slums, with no health care, no education, no nothing. The atrocities have been investigated. There's no real dispute about them. About eighty percent are attributed either to the military or the paramilitaries, who are closely tied to the military.

If you look over the last ten years, you find that within that eighty or seventy-five percent, the percentage attributed to the military has been declining and the percentage attributed to the paramilitaries has been rising. That's for a good reason, a public relations reason. The Colombian army understands as well as everybody else that the best way to carry out terror is by privatizing it. Hand it off to paramilitaries, like the Indonesians did in East Timor, or the Serbs did in Bosnia, and so on. This is pretty standard.

Then you can say you're clean, unless you look at the analyses by academics and reports by human rights organizations like Human Rights Watch, which simply refer to the paramilitaries as the sixth division of the Colombian army, in addition to the five official divisions, the division that's assigned the responsibility for horrendous atrocities in an effort to maintain "plausible deniability," as it's called.

Colombia is also praised. It was praised for its human rights record by Clinton, for example, as a leading democracy, and for its economic reforms. Of those three praises, the third is correct. Colombia has probably the world's record in privatization, that is, handing over its resources to foreign investors. And it is a bonanza for investors. As I've mentioned, part of the privatization is privatization of terror.

And the United States is also privatizing its own contribution to international terrorism, so by now, there are plenty of American advisors in Colombia. But there are probably twice as many U.S. military officers there, technically within private companies like DynCorp and MPRI (Military Professional Resources Inc.). The purpose of that is the same. It's deniability. The privatization of international terrorism means that the advice and arms are free from congressional supervision. There is some congressional legislation that imposes human rights conditions before we can give aid.

The standard way to satisfy them was to issue a waiver. That's what Clinton did: "Well, we're just disregarding them." But Congress added stronger requirements. Now you can't just issue a waiver. So a couple of weeks ago, in early May 2002, Colin Powell determined that Colombia meets Washington's human rights standards, which unfortunately is accurate. If you want to see it, Human Rights Watch/Amnesty International has a detailed report on this. If you can find it, it tells you a lot.

What's the result? Actually, I saw it down in southern Colombia. I was there for a couple of days in Cauca, which had the worst human rights record of any province in the last year. It's quite bad. It's a province mostly of indigenous people, campesinos and Afro-Colombians. They did succeed in organizing what they call a "social bloc," carrying out educational and social and health and other reforms.

They even succeeded, to everybody's astonishment, in electing their own governor, a proud, impressive indigenous man. That's one of the few times in the history of the hemisphere that an indigenous person has been elected to high office. I met him and he is impressive. The consequences of those achievements were the usual ones. Paramilitaries were sent in; they're now spreading over the region. The atrocities are shooting up. Not many people expect the governor to survive his term.

I spent a couple of hours listening to testimonies of poor peasants and they talked about the terror. But the worst terror that they have suffered, at least in the testimonies I heard, is from direct U.S. terror, namely fumigation. Fumigation completely destroys their lives. It destroys their crops, it kills their animals. Children are dying; you can see them with scabs all over their bodies and things like that.

These are poor coffee farmers, mostly. Coffee farming is tricky; prices are low. But they did succeed in carving themselves a niche in the international markets for organically produced high-quality coffee, sold in Germany and places like that. That's gone. Once the coffee trees are destroyed and the land is fumigated and poisoned, it's finished. It's poisoned forever.

Not only are lives destroyed and crops, but biodiversity is also destroyed, and rather crucially, the tradition of peasant agriculture is destroyed. That's a very rich tradition in every part of the world. That's why they have such high yields and so on. A lot of understanding and lore. When that's gone, you can't go back to it.

The fumigation is officially justified as a "war on drugs." This is hard to take seriously except as a cover for a counterinsurgency program, and another stage in the long history of driving peasants off the land for the benefit of wealthy elites and resource extraction by foreign investors.[2]

The consequence is that if this area ever goes back to agriculture, it will be monoculture for agro-export with laboratory-produced seeds, bought from Monsanto. There's no real other alternative. But the main thing is that once the population is driven out by U.S. chemical warfare and crop destruction, then you can open it up for strip mining—apparently there are rich coal fields around—for dams, for hydroelectric power, for international corporations, and so on. So that, too, looks like a success.

As for the people and the cultures and the communities, well, forget about that. They are, to quote a famous philosopher, "mere Things—whose lives are of no value." I'm actually quoting Hegel, speaking on Africans. But that's our attitude. They are mere things whose lives have no value, so therefore we can proceed with this with complete equanimity, and total impunity, and only praise for the achievements.

That's our attitude. They're kind of like the Kurds in southeast Turkey, or the Palestinians. To quote the editor of the *New Republic* on his favorite topic, "The Palestinians will be turned into just another crushed nation, like the Kurds or the Afghans," and the Palestinian problem— "which is beginning to be boring"—will be resolved.

This view was reiterated in May 2002 by the House majority leader, Dick Armey, who gave his solution to the Israel-Palestine problem, namely "the Palestinians should [all] leave." After all, there are plenty of other places in the world, so why don't they just get out, and then the problem will be solved, which is the right way to deal with "mere things" and is, indeed, our attitude toward mere things. Easy to prove. It also helps explain that there is a striking correlation between U.S. military aid and horrible atrocities, including health consequences.

I could go on describing this kind of terror for a long time, but let's turn to another category of terror, that is, economic warfare undertaken in order to crush people's lives. Keeping to the western hemisphere, there are now two countries that are under U.S. embargo. Incidentally, they happen to be the two countries that were leading recipients of slaves, namely Cuba and Haiti.

In the case of Cuba, this has been going on for forty

years. It's part of a much broader campaign of warfare against Cuba. Cuba, as you know, was just renamed by the United States as one of the leading terror states. The reason, presumably, is that it's the leading target of international terrorism for the last forty years, maybe more than the rest of the world combined. Maybe Lebanon is up there somewhere.

The warfare against Cuba has gone on since 1959. The pretext up until 1989 was that we had to defend ourselves from this tentacle of the Russian empire, which was about to strangle us, so therefore we had to support terror and economic warfare. In 1989, that pretext lost its place, and instantly, without batting an eyelash, we shifted to another pretext. The earlier one was forgotten, and the embargo got harsher. And it was because of our love of democracy, it turned out.

Ever since then, we've been carrying out economic warfare and supporting terror against Cuba, because of our love of democracy, as demonstrated in countries like, say, Colombia. Colombia actually did allow an independent party a couple of years ago, and it was even allowed to run in an election, which was a little difficult because within a couple of years, three thousand of its leading figures were murdered by death squads connected to the U.S.-backed military, including presidential candidates and mayors and so on. But it's still a great democracy compared to, say, Cuba. I won't go on.

The embargo is unusually severe, in fact unique, in that it effectively bars food and medicines in violation of every imaginable humanitarian law. It is condemned by the whole world. The shift from defending ourselves against Cuban attack as an outpost of the Russian empire to our love of democracy took place without notice. You can check back and see how many people commented on this sudden change.

And that makes sense because the fear of Communism was always a total fraud. We know that and have known it for years from the declassified internal record. It's from the Kennedy administration. I suppose that's why it's never cited. Historian Arthur Schlesinger submitted secret reports to Kennedy analyzing this, and they're quite revealing. (I've written about this in my book *Profit over People.*)

The effect of the Cuban embargo, the standard line here, which was repeated by former President Carter a couple of weeks ago, is that the embargo helps Castro and, of course, doesn't harm the Cubans. The only people who are harmed by it are North Americans like farmers and agro-business who want to export there, but it has no effect on Cuba except to help Castro.

There are other people who have looked at the situation, like the American Association of World Health, which did a detailed study in March 1997. They published three hundred pages of documentation and concluded that the embargo had dramatically harmed health and nutrition in Cuba, and caused a significant rise in suffering and death. It would have been a humanitarian catastrophe, they said, except that it was averted by the Cuban health system, which is quite astonishing, though it did direct resources in the health system away from other needs, with the obvious consequences.

So the embargo has been a success, like the U.S. Army's defeat of liberation theology. Well, that's one of the two embargoes. The other is possibly more grotesque; that's Haiti. Haiti has been the main target of U.S. military intervention and other intervention for the last century. It's now the poorest country in the hemisphere. It may not survive another generation or two, another correlation you might want to think about that actually generalizes.

Haiti was invaded by Woodrow Wilson in what's called "an exercise of Wilsonian idealism," if you studied international relations theory. The Marines invaded it in 1915, destroyed the parliamentary system, reinstituted slavery, killed nobody knows how many people (Haitians say about fifteen thousand), turned their country into a plantation for U.S. investors, and instituted a National Guard, which is a brutal, murderous force that has run the place pretty much ever since under U.S. backing.

I won't run through the whole history, but this continued right through the mid-1990s when Bush and Clinton supported the military junta directly, right through the worst terror. That was another thing that I saw personally for a couple of days. Right now, nearby here, in Queens, New York, one of their leading criminals, Emmanuel Constant, is hidden by the United States. He's already been sentenced in Haiti for terrorist crimes. He was the head of the paramilitary force that was responsible for killing maybe four or five thousand people in Haiti in the early 1990s when Bush and Clinton were supporting the military junta.

Haiti has tried to extradite him, but of course the United States doesn't even bother responding, and the press won't even comment on it. Why should we extradite a major killer who's only involved in killing a couple of thousand people, especially because if he goes back he'll probably spill the beans about direct U.S. connections to the terror that was going on at the time. And again, that elicits no comment.

There is medical commentary on this, primarily by Paul Farmer, who has written about this subject recently. By 1995, after the junta was finally thrown out, the Inter-American Development Bank (IADB) and other agencies began projects to try to rebuild what was left of the battered public health system, but that has been stopped. They wanted to try to reverse the decline of life expectancy, the only case of that in this hemisphere.

That effort was stopped by the embargo. It blocked half a billion dollars' worth of aid that was coming from the IADB and other sources, and it terminated the projects and, of course, exacerbated the already horrendous conditions. The only help they're getting is from Cuba, as in the case of many other poor countries, including direct assistance from a lot of Cuban medical personnel, but they can't compensate for the losses.

Haiti, incidentally, is paying interest on the loans that are blocked and that it isn't receiving, just to add to the catastrophe. So that's the second embargo. This is also being imposed because of our love of democracy, as Powell and others have explained.

Well, without going on, there is actually an interesting and rather flourishing literary genre in the United States now, with best-selling books and articles, which is focusing on a strange flaw in our character, namely: Why don't we respond properly to the crimes of others? There are major books on this, and it's kind of an interesting topic. It might merit a footnote in a study of our attitude toward human rights, a footnote where the main topic, of course, would be a different one, namely: Why do we keep participating crucially in human rights violations of the most severe kind, including atrocities?

But that's an unaskable question. You can ask about our inadequacy in responding to the crimes of others. But you can't ask questions about anything that I've been talking about, about our own massive crimes, because that would be to concede that there are such crimes, and that's inconceivable. How could that be? If you try to raise that question, you're kind of off the spectrum somewhere.

Similarly, there is plenty of grave commentary these days on what we should do to combat the plague of terror, and it is serious. There are dangerous terrorist threats all over. There is actually one simple way for the United States to decrease very significantly the amount of terror in the world, and that is to just stop supporting and participating in it. That would have a major effect right there. I mean, it wouldn't solve everything, but a big piece of it would be gone. However, you'll search in vain for any discussion of that elementary point.

Well, until questions of this kind move into the agenda, in fact, become the center of attention, discussion of topics of this nature can't really be taken very seriously, and suffering people throughout the world will simply sink deeper into misery.

♦ ♦ ♦

[The following is an excerpt from the question-and-answer session after Chomsky's talk.]

Q: I think, and I hope you'll agree, that what was radically different between what the Nazis did and what we did in Vietnam was the intent. The Nazis intended to exterminate the Jewish population of Europe. The intent in Vietnam was not genocide.

CHOMSKY: I'd never call what happened in Vietnam genocide. That's not the right term for it. I agree, it was totally different. I can't recall anyone suggesting otherwise. Actually, it's different in all sorts of respects. The Nazis really are historically unique. There have been a lot of atrocities in human history, but industrialized mass extermination of the style that the Nazis carried out is off the spectrum. There's just nothing that compares to it. The Jews and the Roma, the people we call Gypsies, were treated about the same way, and some other groups. That was unique.

But there are plenty of atrocities in the world, and a lot of them trace right back to us. And a lot of them aren't even counted. Let me give you an example that isn't counted. You'll remember, I'm sure, a book that came out and was a big best-seller about a year ago called *The Black Book of Communism*. There were prominent reviews in the *New York Times*, all over the place. It was a translation of a French book, which estimated the number of people killed by the Communists at one hundred million. Well, without quibbling about the numbers, let's say that's right.

The biggest component of that was a famine in China from 1958 to 1960, which is estimated to have killed about twenty-five million people. The reason why that's called a political crime—an ideological crime—which is a good reason in my opinion, was discussed in most detail by Amartya Sen; it's part of the work for which he won the Nobel Prize. Sen is an economist who treated this as an ideological crime for good reasons. He said it wasn't a matter of intent; they didn't intend to kill anybody. It's just that the ideological institutions were such that it happened. It was a totalitarian state where no information about what was happening ever got back to the center. They couldn't take any action because that's what happens in a totalitarian state. So it was a reflection of the totalitarian institutions, a huge massacre that wasn't intended. They didn't intend to kill twenty-five million people, but it was still a major massacre, and it's correct to call it one of the major atrocities of the twentieth century, and the worst single component of the crimes of Communism. That's accurate.

That bears on your question of intent. But that's only half the story. If you look at Amartya Sen's work, for which he won the Nobel Prize and for which he's famous academically, he studied famines and the conditions that lead to them. And as a major part of this, he compared India and China. Of course, India, while it was under British rule, had huge famines all the time, with tens of millions of people dying, but nobody counts that among the crimes of British imperialism because, again, when we do it, it's not a crime.

But starting from independence, as Sen points out, India had plenty of starvation, but it didn't have major famines of that kind. From 1947 until the time when he did the work for which he won the Nobel Prize, around 1980, there were no major famines. He compares that with China, which did have this one major famine, and he points to a difference in institutions between the two countries. In India, which was democratic, if information appeared about hunger somewhere, the central authorities could do something about it, so there weren't major famines.

That's part of what he wrote. That part is known all over the place. But then he continued. Here's the rest, from the same articles and the same books, but not known. He then said, Well, let's compare the death rates in China and India from 1947 until the time he wrote. They were approximately the same around 1947, similar countries, and so on. The mortality rate started to decline in China pretty sharply; it stayed very high in India. And he regards that as an ideological crime, too.

He says the difference is that China instituted rural health clinics, preventive medicine for the poor, and so on, and this led to a significant improvement in health standards, so you get a decline in mortality rates. India didn't. It was a democratic capitalist country, in which you don't do anything for poor people. And he then points out that if you take a look at the difference between those curves, let me just quote him, he says, "India seems to manage to fill its cupboard with more skeletons every eight years than China put there in its years of shame [1958–61]."

That comes to about one hundred million people in

India alone from 1947 to 1980. But we don't call that a crime of democratic capitalism. If we were to carry out that calculation throughout the world...I won't even talk about it. But Sen is correct; they're not intended, just like the Chinese famine wasn't intended. But they are ideological and institutional crimes, and capitalist democracy and its advocates are responsible for them, in whatever sense supporters of so-called Communism are responsible for the Chinese famine. We don't have the entire responsibility, but certainly a large part of it.

So, yes, if you count crimes, it's an ugly record, but it's only the enemy's crimes that count. They're the ones that we deplore and agonize about, and so on. Our own, which may be monstrously worse, they just don't enter into our field of vision. You don't study them, you don't read about them, you don't think about them, nobody writes about them. We're just not allowed to think about them, and if we agree to that, that's our choice.

NOTES

1. See 'W' and Torture: Two Trial Observations, Sept. 2002, published by the Kurdish Human Rights Project (London), the Bar Human Rights Committee of England and Wales, the Human Rights Association (Ankara), section 2, "the 'W' Case." Technically, the Turkish spelling is "Nevruz" and the Kurdish spelling is "Newroz."

2. See Doug Stokes, "Better Lead than Bread? A Critical Analysis of the U.S.'s Plan Colombia," Civil Wars 4.2 (summer 2001), 59–78; Garry M. Leech, Killing Peace (Information Network of the Americas, NY, 2002, 66f. For background and further discussion, Chomsky, Rogue States, chapter 5.)

PART III

Talks and Conversations

"Why Do They Hate Us,
When We're So Good?"

An excerpt from "Peering into the Abyss of the Future," a talk given to benefit the Peninsula Peace and Justice Center, Rickey's Hyatt House, Palo Alto, California, March 22, 2002.

AFTER SEPTEMBER 11, SOME OF THE PRESS, particularly the *Wall Street Journal*, did do what they should have done: they began investigating opinion in the [Middle East] region. They were trying to find out the answer to George Bush's plaintive question: "Why do they hate us, when we're so good?" How can that be?

Actually, even before he asked the question, the *Wall Street Journal* had provided some of the answers. They focused their survey of opinion in the region on the people they care about, what they called "moneyed Muslims," meaning bankers, lawyers, managers of branches of U.S. transnationals—those kind of people. People who are right inside the U.S. system and of course, naturally despise Osama bin Laden, if only because they are his main targets—they're the ones he's after, so they don't like him.

And in that group, what's their opinion about the

United States? Well, it turns out they're very antagonistic to U.S. policy. The main policies they're just part of—like the international economic policies. But what they object to is the fact that the United States has consistently opposed democracy and independent development, and is supporting corrupt, brutal regimes. Naturally, they're strongly opposed to the unilateral U.S. support for the Israeli military occupation, which is very harsh and brutal, and is now in its thirty-fifth year. They strongly oppose the U.S. sanctions against Iraq, which they understand perfectly well and you know, too, are devastating the population but strengthening Saddam Hussein.

And they remember another thing that we like to forget: that the United States and Britain supported Saddam Hussein right through his worst atrocities, continued to help him develop weapons of mass destruction, didn't do anything to stop him from gassing Kurds or anything else. They remember that, even if we choose to sweep it under the carpet. And for reasons like that, they say they have a lot of hatred for U.S. policies, despite the fact that they're right in the middle of the entire U.S. system. Well, that's one answer to George Bush's question. It's not the kind of answer you read in most of the intellectual journals and the press. There you read sophisticated answers about how people in that region have "bad cultures," or they are left out by globalization, or they can't stand our freedoms and our magnificence, and so on and so forth.

Anyone who is seriously concerned with these issues, certainly anyone who's a specialist in international affairs or the Middle East, knows there's nothing new about these answers. You can go way back and find them, as far back as you want to go. One of the advantages of living here is that the United States has become, over the years, a very free country. Not as a gift from the gods, but, as the result of plenty of popular struggle, it's become an unusually free country, uniquely so in some respects. We have more information about high-level U.S. policy planning than you can find in any country in the world that I know about, including tons of declassified material that shows how policy is being conducted and what the government's thinking is.

Well, the obvious place to look, if you want to find out more about this, is the records for 1958. Nineteen fifty-eight was a critical year in U.S. international affairs, for a lot of reasons. In particular with regard to the Middle East, it was a critical year because it was the first year in which some country, namely Iraq, had been able to break out of the Anglo-American condominium over the world's energy resources. A conservative nationalist regime in Iran had tried, but there was a U.S.-British military coup that overthrew it.

Iraq actually broke out, and it was a huge issue, with a big flurry of activity and military forces all over the place, which almost saw the use of nuclear weapons. It was an enormous issue. So if you want to understand what the United States was thinking about, you look back to those records.

Well, if you do, you find that President Eisenhower, in internal discussion, observed to his staff, in his words, that there's "a campaign of hatred against us" in the Arab world, "not by the governments but by the people." And there was discussion about this. The National Security Council, the highest planning body, gave their analysis. They said that the reason is that there's a perception in the region that the United States is supporting harsh, brutal, and corrupt regimes, and is blocking democratization and development, and is doing so because of our interest in controlling the oil reserves of the region.

And they said it's difficult to counter this perception because it's accurate. Not only is it accurate but it should be accurate. They said that it is natural for us to support status quo governments, meaning the kind I just described, and to prevent democracy and development, because we want to maintain control over the energy resources of the region.

So there's a campaign of hatred against us by the people, and that's the reason for it. Essentially the same as what the *Wall Street Journal* discovered on September 14, 2001, and anybody knew in between. The only difference is that, of course, some of the specific policies, like the sanctions against Iraq, are new, and so on. But the general policies are the same.

And among the people, there's a much deeper resentment because they don't see any particular reason why the wealth of the region should flow to the West and to the moneyed Muslims, who are cooperating with the West, and not to them. It reflects a kind of backward culture, as you read in commentary in the United States. The idea somehow hadn't penetrated people's minds. It still hasn't. So there's an even deeper campaign of hatred among the people who aren't moneyed Muslims in the middle of the U.S. system.

So if you want to listen to some voices outside the cocoon, it's not hard to hear them, and they'll answer the questions about why there's a campaign of hatred against us, whether it's now or in 1958, and in a good part of the rest of the world where people just don't enjoy being ground to dust under somebody's boot. They don't like it, and it leads to hatred. You can indulge in the fantasies if you like, but that's a choice. You certainly don't have to.

Visiting the West Bank with Azmi Bishara

An excerpt from a talk given to benefit the legal defense of Azmi Bishara, an Israeli Arab member of the Knesset and a friend of Chomsky's for many years. The talk took place at Hunter College, New York City, on May 25, 2002.

THE IMMEDIATE OCCASION FOR OUR BEING here tonight is the lifting of Azmi Bishara's immunity and the charges for which he is facing trial: primarily his assertion that people in Lebanon had the right to resist a foreign occupation and to drive the occupying army out of their country; his call for supporting the current intifada as an alternative to the other possible choices, namely either total submission or going to war; and his involvement in efforts at family reunification.

Azmi's position on this, which he has stated forthrightly, is that he has asked people not to look at it as an issue of freedom of speech, although, of course, it is that. Rather, he is calling on people to say openly and forthrightly that what he said is correct, not just that he has a right to say it, but that what he said was accurate. And he has strong grounds for that.

He also added another point. He said that the issue is not what he said, but rather that he was the person who said it. The condemnation of Azmi is an attack on the right of Israeli Arabs to take an independent political position. This conclusion was supported by the reaction to physical attacks against Azmi that took place in October 2000 (remember this was under the Barak government, with the "peace camp" as part of it). At that time in October, three hundred people attacked his house and Azmi was wounded by police fire. During this same time thirteen Israeli Arabs were killed, several by the police. All of this happened with complete impunity. The Israeli peace camp, including well-known intellectuals who are regarded—here at least, if not in Israel—as the conscience of Israel, refused to give him support.

After these events, the speaker of the Knesset, whose responsibility it is to defend the Knesset, never said a word. There was never any reaction. And as Azmi wrote, this created a sharp moral barrier, separating his supporters in Israel (and there were some) and Palestinian Arabs and him from those who call themselves the peace camp. I think he's correct about that as well.

Azmi has always expressed great respect for Israeli democracy, which is unique in the region, and for the cultural and social achievements that have been part of what he calls "the construction of the Hebrew nation." But it's for Israeli Jews. Arab citizens of Israel are, at best, tolerated. There is no need to run though the history of this, which is not getting any prettier.

Let me just add a personal note about a trip that I made

through the West Bank in 1988. I mention it partly because it relates to Azmi and partly because I think it has a significant bearing on current issues. I wrote about this trip, first in the Hebrew press in Israel and then in the United States. Parts of these accounts are included in the new edition of my book *Fateful Triangle*, which came out several years ago.

At the time, I did not mention who my companion was; it was Azmi. I didn't mention it, for the usual reasons: one does not mention the names of vulnerable people in countries that are suffering severe repression. But I guess now it's okay after these years and after what's happened. So I will mention it.

I met Azmi for the first time at 6:00 A.M. on a day in April 1988. That was at a demonstration outside the Dahariya Prison, which was known as "the slaughterhouse." It was a way station to the prison at Ketziot in the Negev, which is a horrible torture chamber, usually called Ansar III. Ansar I was the huge and horrifying torture chamber in southern Lebanon. This was also reported at the time, but its nature has been exposed since the Israeli forces abandoned the country. There was also an Ansar II in Gaza. Ansar III was the place that you went after the slaughterhouse in Dahariya.

The town nearby was under siege at the time. The demonstration was made up of Israelis and a number of foreign visitors who were at an academic conference, which I happened to be attending too. Interesting things happened there, but I'll go on.

After the demonstration, we piled into Azmi's car and

he drove me through the West Bank. We spent the rest of the day there, starting in Nablus, where we went to the Old City and talked to activists in the Casbah. Anyone who's been there can only have extra-painful images of what's happened recently. You couldn't drive a car through those streets, let alone a tank.

The reports from Nablus are even more grim than what's been reported from Jenin: the large-scale terrible destruction, with plenty of killing and all of the usual horrors that you've read about. In the case of Nablus, this means destruction of historical treasures going back to Roman times, in addition to what's happened to the people.

Anyway, in 1988, after Nablus, we went through villages in the West Bank, many of them under attack. Some we had to leave as army forces were coming in, because local villagers wanted us to get out of there. They were worried about what would happen if foreigners were found there, having had ugly experiences with that before.

Of all the villages we went to, the most dramatic case was the village that had become famous a couple of days earlier, namely Beita. Beita is a traditional conservative village nestled in the hills not too far from Ramallah. I don't think many people even knew that it was there. It clearly had been a very attractive place, with old houses, hundreds of years old.

Right after the first intifada started, Beita declared itself liberated. That led to an attack by the Israeli occupying forces. When we got there, the village was under military siege, but it was possible, with the help of lawyers from Al-Haq (Law in the Service of Man) in Ramallah, to get into it over back roads, climbing over hills with the help of neighboring villagers. We spent a couple of hours there before the 7:00 P.M. curfew came, at which time you really had to get out or your life was in danger. So we got out over the roads.

At that time Beita, as some of you will remember, had been attacked and partially destroyed by Israeli forces. The reason—and the reason for the tight military siege—was that a group of Israeli hikers, from a nearby Israeli settlement, Elon Moreh, had entered the fields of Beita. They were led by a man named Romam Aldubi, who was a criminal extremist—in fact, the only Jew ever to have been barred by the military authorities from entering any Arab areas. The hikers found a shepherd in the field and killed him. They were brought into the village, where they killed a couple of other people.

Following that, the mother of one of the people who was killed threw a stone at Aldubi, and he fired and killed an Israeli girl, Tirza Porat, who was one of the hikers. That led to a hysterical reaction in Israel, including calls to destroy the town and to drive the whole population out. The Israeli army knew exactly what had happened, and told people. But for whatever reason, maybe to cut back on a more serious reaction among the settlers, the army went into the town and smashed it up.

The official story was that they destroyed fifteen buildings and homes, after giving people ample warning to leave. That was a total lie. The number of homes that were destroyed, as we could see, was at least twice that, and it was obvious that nobody had been given any time to leave. People were rummaging around the wreckage trying to find possessions and so on.

Several people from the town were in jail, including the mother and the pregnant sister of one of the murdered men. Later, half a dozen people were expelled from the country; others stayed in jail. Though it was well known that Aldubi was the killer both of the Palestinians and of the Israeli girl, he was never punished, although he did come to trial. The authorities determined that the tragic events that had happened were already punishment enough for him. So it was only the people in the village who had to be punished, and they were.

That's pretty standard in a lot of such cases, running right to the present. At the time we were there—it happened to be a bitter cold, rainy day, as happens in that season, April—the people whose houses were demolished were living outdoors, trying to cook outdoors and so on. It was a pretty ugly and painful scene. Their attitudes were striking. They were not resigned. They were quiet and determined. We asked them whether they would be willing to accept assistance from Israeli Jews to rebuild what they had destroyed, and they told us that they would, under certain conditions. If the assistance was given honestly, they would accept it happily. If it was given as an effort to create an image of what's called "the beautiful Israel," a term that's used in Israel in Hebrew as a term of contempt for a disgraceful posture that's familiar, they didn't want anything to do with it. Strikingly, there was no call for revenge or any retaliation, just the quiet determination to continue.

I saw the same thing a day or two later in Ramallah. It was also necessary to get there through back roads; it too was under siege. When I got there, with an Israeli and an Arab friend, the town was strangely quiet. We walked through the town, got to the Ramallah hospital, and walked in. There was no staff, no nurses, no doctors, no attendants, but plenty of people. The reason, we discovered, was that there had been some disruption outside with a heavy army presence, and the staff had been warned to stay away. The beds were all full, the usual hospital scene: IVs coming out of arms and that sort of business. They described to us what had happened to them, some of them children, some older. They had suffered atrocities during the Israeli suppression of the intifada, and it was the same thing. Quiet determination. No word about retaliation or revenge.

All of this reveals a very remarkable fact about the military occupation. It went on for thirty-four years and was harsh, brutal, and repressive from the beginning, with robbery of land and resources. But there was no retaliation, not from the occupied territories. Israel was immune from any attack from within the territories. There was some from outside, including atrocities, though they were a fraction of Israel's own atrocities. And when I refer to Israel, I mean the United States and Israel, because everything that Israel does is done up to the limits that the United States supports and authorizes. So it's U.S.-Israeli atrocities.

That's why the events of the last year are such a shock. The United States and Israel have lost the complete monopoly on violence. They still have an overwhelming preponderance, but not a monopoly. That's shocking. September 11 was exactly the same, but on a global scale. September 11 was a horrible atrocity, but it wasn't new. There are plenty of atrocities like that. It's only that they take place somewhere else.

NOTE

1. In an unprecedented move, the Knesset lifted Bishara's parliamentary immunity in November 2001, opening the way for his indictment by the Israeli attorney general on two charges. The first, an alleged violation of the Prevention of Terror Ordinance, concerned two public speeches made by Bishara in which he affirmed the right of occupied peoples to resist occupation. The second charge, violation of 1948 emergency regulations on foreign travel, concerned Bishara's arrangement of humanitarian visits for elderly Palestinian citizens of Israel to unite with refugee relatives in Syria.

Media Bias and Palestine

An excerpt from a small-group discussion after Chomsky's talk in Palo Alto, California, March 22, 2002.

Q: Do you have any concern that CNN and MSNBC are becoming mouthpieces for the U.S. military?

CHOMSKY: They're much less so than they were in the past. So it's not they're becoming, they always were, and it's less so than it used to be. Take MSNBC. Since September 11, the media, at least the commercial media, not so much NPR and PBS, but the commercial media have opened up somewhat. For example, I was at MSNBC for a long discussion program in November 2001 for the first time ever, and other people too. Mike Albert was on for an hour. Howard Zinn's been on. This kind of thing never happened before. It's a reflection of public concerns that are forcing the media to open up a little.

I hope you're right. I tend to be a little skeptical.

You should be. The concentration of the media is taking place, but there are other pressures that I think are more important.

Why? What's the mechanism by which the government influences the media?

It doesn't. The government has almost no influence over the media.

How does that happen, then? What's the underlying mechanism?

It's kind of like asking, How does the government convince General Motors to try to increase profit? It doesn't make any sense. The media are huge corporations that share the interests of the corporate sector that dominates the government. The government can't tell the media what to do because they don't have the power to do it here. In this respect, the United States is unusually free. Like, in England, the government can raid the office of the BBC and stop them from doing things. They can't do it here.

Okay, we've won a kind of freedom that England doesn't have. So the government has almost no influence on the media. If the media decide to do something, it's their own decision.

So what prevents something like East Timor or other issues from arising? Why isn't there more dissent in the media? Is it just that people don't want to hear it, so they're not going to make money?

Why should a major corporation be interested in exposing the fact that they're involved in genocide?

They're not. It's the U.S. government.

They're part of the system that runs the U.S. government. They share the interest in having Indonesia as the major source of resources that we're going to exploit, and being a powerful force that will dominate that region. It's the same as the one in Washington. So why should they expose it? And in particular, why should they expose the fact that they themselves share responsibility for the slaughter of people by hundreds of thousands. The same reason they didn't report on Turkey the last couple of years. It's not in their interests.

Let me give you a simple example. The current intifada in the occupied territories started on September 29, 2000. On October 1, two days later, Israel started using U.S. helicopters—there are no Israeli helicopters—to attack civilian targets, apartment complexes and so on, killing and wounding dozens of people. That went on for two days. No Palestinian fire, just stone-throwing from kids. On October 3, after two days of this, Clinton made the biggest deal in a decade to send military helicopters to Israel. The media here refused to publish it. To this day, there has not been a report.

That was a decision of editors. I happen to know some of the editors of the *Boston Globe*. I've been living there for more than forty-five years. I actually joined with a group that went and talked to them, and they simply made it clear, they're not going to publish it. And the same decision was made by every other newspaper in the United States, literally every one. Somebody did a database search. The only reference to it in the country he could find was a letter in Raleigh, North Carolina.

Now, did the government tell them not to publish this story? No. If it had told them not to, they probably would have published it, just out of indignation. But they just realize it's not in their interest to say that as soon as a U.S. military base—which is, to a large extent, what Israel has chosen to be—begins using U.S. helicopters to murder civilians, we send them more helicopters. It's not in the interest of the editorial offices to do that, so they don't.

That happens to be an unusually narrow and easily identifiable case. But it generalizes.

You said the United States tries to block the Middle East peace. First, why do you say that, since Clinton looked like he was trying to make progress?

He was trying to make progress, which almost reached the level of South Africa forty years ago, but not quite.

What's the motive?

The motive is that Israel is a U.S. military base. And it's strong. It's one of the states that, like Turkey, controls the Middle East region militarily in the interest of the United States. And the Palestinians offer nothing. They don't have any power, they don't have any wealth, so they don't have any rights.

Isn't it still better to have a peace rather than all of this?

That depends on what kind of peace it is. Ultimately the United States might agree to what South Africa agreed to forty years ago. South Africa not only agreed, they initiated the establishment of black states—the Bantustans. And it is conceivable that sooner or later the United States might rise to the level of South Africa in the darkest days of apartheid and allow a Palestinian Bantustan in the occupied territories. I wouldn't be surprised. I think that, from their point of view, it would be smart for them to do that.

Does it mean anything?

Not much. It means pretty much what Transkei meant. Will they allow a really independent state? No, probably, because that will interfere with their own power. Israel is an offshore base for U.S. power. If it stopped being that, the United States would throw them in the drink with everyone else. But as long as they're an offshore base for the extension of U.S. power, they can do what they want.

So that means that what Clinton did was a fake thing.

It wasn't fake. Did you ever see a map of the Clinton plan? There's a good reason for that. In the entire American press, they never published a map. The reason is, as soon as you look at the maps, you see what was going on. The Clinton plan was going to break the West Bank into four separate cantons, largely separated from one another. East Jerusalem, which is one of the cantons, is the center of Palestinian life. It's separate from all the others. This is also all separate from the Gaza Strip, which itself is broken up into cantons. It didn't even rise to the level of South Africa in the days of the Bantustans.That is why they didn't publish any maps.

How is Israel serving the interests of the United States?

There's a long history of this. But to go back to 1958, the year I mentioned in my talk, at that point U.S. intelligence said that support for Israel as a base for U.S. power is a "logical corollary" of their opposition to independent Arab nationalism, because Israel can be a force like Turkey, like Iran under the Shah, that will control and repress independent forces in the Arab countries. The United States didn't do anything about it then.

In 1967, Israel performed a major service, smashed Arab nationalism, destroyed Nasser, who was at the center of the whole secular nationalist movement, which really was a threat to the rule by the Saudi Arabian elite. At that point, the alliance with the United States firmed up, and precisely at that point, Israel became the darling of American liberal intellectuals. Before that, they didn't care much about Israel.

Haven't things changed since then?

Yeah, it became worse, in 1970, during Black September. Remember, it looked for a while as if Syria might make a move to protect Palestinians who were being slaughtered in Jordan. The United States didn't want that, but the U.S. government was mired in Cambodia—the whole country was blowing up—and they couldn't send military forces to do anything. They asked Israel to intervene by mobilizing the air force—meaning the adjunct of the U.S. Air Force—to prevent Syria from moving. They did it, Syria backed off, Palestinians were slaughtered, and U.S. aid to Israel quadrupled. This continued through the 1970s.

In 1979, the Shah, a major pillar of U.S. power, fell, and Israel's role became more important. And it continues right to the present. The main Egyptian newspaper had a big article called "Axis of Evil" recently. They said there really is an "Axis of Evil": the United States, Israel, and Turkey. It's an axis of evil aimed at the Arab states, and has been for years, a tight alliance, with joint military maneuvers all over the place. Israel is the most reliable and strongest base. By now it's so integrated into the U.S. military economy, it's indistinguishable.

So it's of great value. In contrast to the Palestinians, who are of no value. The Palestinians are of as much value to the U.S. government as the people of Rwanda.

Don't you think it's spoiling relations with some of the Arab states that would otherwise be close to the United States?

That's exactly why Washington ordered Sharon, very politely, to pull the tanks and soldiers out of the Palestinian cities, because it was interfering with Dick Cheney's mission. Well, the master speaks, the servant obeys. So within minutes, they had pulled out. But don't forget, the leaders of the Arab states are at some level pro-Israel, because they understand that Israel is part of the system protecting them from their own people.

And they'd like to have an excuse to be more supportive of U.S. policy, if only Israel would let them.

They'd like them to tone it down. Not kill so many people. Ultimately, in that region, everything is about oil.

How Should We Respond?

This section contains several discussions about tactics of resistance from the question-and-answer session after the Palo Alto talk and after a talk given to benefit the Middle Eastern Children's Alliance, at the Berkeley Community Theater, on March 21, 2002.

Q: Thanks again, Professor Chomsky, for giving the talk. My question relates to something you alluded to a little earlier, when you talked about Haiti. This summer I had a chance to hear a speech from General Romeo Dallaire, who is in charge of the UN mission in Rwanda, about how frustrated he was to watch genocide happen all around him when no one seemed to care, none of the world powers seemed to be doing anything. And his basic conclusion was that to him the world was just inherently a racist place, that it allowed such things to happen. And I was curious if you could comment on his rather pessimistic conclusion, if you agree with that assessment or if it should be qualified in some sense.

CHOMSKY: First of all, I don't think what happened was racism, particularly. It's just that this didn't matter much. Remember, he was talking about what happened in Rwanda in 1994, but that's been going on in Burundi and Rwanda for years. Ed Herman and I wrote a book more than twenty-three years ago in which we discussed the Hutu/Tutsi atrocities in Burundi and Rwanda, in which hundreds of thousands of people were killed. Nobody cared then, and nobody cares now. Just like in the last two or three years, probably several million people have been killed in the Congo, and it doesn't really matter, it doesn't affect Western interests, so you don't try to do anything about it.

But they can be any color, any religion, it doesn't really matter. The principle is, does it affect U.S. interests? If you take a look at the Kurds I was talking about, they're Aryan, if anybody cares. If they walked around the streets, we'd see more Aryans, maybe with slightly darker skin, but we wouldn't notice. But if they get slaughtered, that's fine. It's not like Dallaire. He's talking about something bad, namely our unwillingness to do anything to stop atrocities. But much worse than that, incomparably worse, is our willingness to participate in atrocities. It would have been much worse if we had not only done nothing about that, but in fact had gone ahead and continued to put the guns in the hands of the murderers as they were committing murder.

I'd be a little cautious. The kind of statement he's making is correct, but that's the kind that's tolerable. So, for example, if you take a look at the *New York Review of Books* this week, there's a passionate article by the executive director of the Carr Center for Human Rights Policy at Harvard's Kennedy School of Government, Samantha Power, which discusses our tragic failure to pay attention to atrocities that other people are committing and to do something about them. It's some profound flaw in our character. Okay, it's a problem.

But a much more serious problem, orders of magnitude more serious—which is not mentioned in the article and which would be unintelligible if it were mentioned—is the fact that we pay very close attention to atrocities and intervene to escalate them, and often even applaud them. The case of Turkey is only one example. No such examples are mentioned in the article, and couldn't be. If you wrote an article about that, you wouldn't get it published, and if you did, nobody would understand it, at least nobody with a good education. And that's the important point.

Yeah, it's bad to overlook the crimes that are committed by others and not to do enough about them, but it's far more important to look into the mirror and look at what you're doing yourself, and do something about that. So I kind of agree with Dallaire. It seems to me a bad problem, but small on the scale of moral responsibilities or human consequences.

You've said that we as citizens should not speak truth to power but, instead, to people. Shouldn't we do both? Could you speak more on this subject?

This is a reference to perhaps the only thing on which I find I disagree with my Quaker friends. On every practical activity I usually agree with them, but I do disagree with them about their slogan of speaking truth to power. First of all, power already knows the truth. They don't need to hear it from us. Secondly, it's a waste of time. Furthermore, it's the wrong audience. You have to speak truth to the people who will dismantle and overthrow and constrain power. Furthermore, I don't like the phrase "speak truth to." We don't know the truth. At least I don't.

We should join with the kind of people who are willing to commit themselves to overthrow power, and listen to them. They often know a lot more than we do. And join with them to carry out the right kinds of activities. Should you also speak truth to power? If you feel like it, but I don't see a lot of point. I'm not interested in telling the people around Bush what they already know.

I've considered not paying my taxes, to protest the use of our tax dollars to fund our government's military actions. What do you think of this?

Well, as I've said before, I never trust my own tactical judgment. Just to give my own experience, back in 1965, along with a couple of friends, I did try to organize a national tax resistance movement. I can't claim it was overwhelmingly successful, it wasn't, but quite a fair number of us didn't pay taxes for quite a few years, in my case about ten years. I don't know if it was effective or not, I just can't judge. I know what happened to some.

The government responds, in what looks like a random way. In some cases, they will go after you. I know cases where they went after people, took their houses and possessions, and so on. In my personal case, it was mostly a matter of sending passionate letters to the IRS, which were read by some computer that returned to me a form letter that said whatever it said. Since there's no way, in my case, not to pay taxes, they can go right to the source of the salary, which they did, and take the taxes, plus a penalty, so they got the taxes. And they didn't do anything more. But in some cases they did.

How much effect it had on policy and what it would be if there was really a massive tax-resistance movement, which we were unable to develop, I just don't know. These are hard, tactical judgments, I don't have any particular insight. I don't trust my own advice, and there's no reason why you should.

I want to also thank you for sharing your enlightening information about the many criminal acts that have been conducted on behalf of our country, and it seems like in this room there are a lot of people who are very focused on action. And in light of what you've said here tonight and in light of what we know has gone on in Afghanistan, perhaps one of the actions that we have in front of us is divestiture in the companies that are sponsoring the proliferation of weapons, that are helping to create and build the ethnic tension and create atrocity after atrocity.

So, I wanted to ask you whether this subject of divestiture or action in this realm has been discussed elsewhere.

Yeah, it's being discussed, it surely has been, and should be. It's a tactical question, by which I don't mean a minor question, but a question of huge significance. It's the tactical questions that have human consequences. But these are delicate judgments. You have to try to figure out what's the consequence of carrying out this act under existing circumstances, and who will you reach, and how will people understand it, and will it be the basis for an organizing effort that will go on to something else, and so on.

Such campaigns have sometimes been successful. In the case of South Africa, there were similar campaigns, and they had an effect on U.S. policy. Remember what U.S. policy was—this is one of the things that's swept under the rug, so let me remind you. In 1988, not that long ago, Nelson Mandela's African National Congress was an officially designated terrorist organization, in fact worse than that. The State Department listed it as one of the "more notorious terrorist groups." In the same year, 1988, South Africa was welcomed as a favored ally. Just in the Reagan years alone, the 1980s, South Africa killed about a million and a half people in the surrounding countries, not inside South Africa, and caused about sixty billion dollars of damage, with action supported by the United States and Britain.

That was 1988. In fact, in December 1987 the United Nations passed its major resolution condemning terrorism in all its forms, and called on all countries of the world to do everything they could to stamp out this terrible plague. It didn't pass unanimously. One country abstained, namely Honduras, and two countries voted against it, namely the United States and Israel. When the United States votes against a resolution, it's not reported and it disappears from history, which is what happened to the major UN resolution against terrorism.

And the two negative voters explained why. There was a paragraph in the resolution which said that "nothing in the present resolution could in any way prejudice the right to self-determination, freedom and independence, as derived from the Charter of the United Nations, of peoples forcibly deprived of that right...particularly peoples under colonial and racist regimes and foreign occupation or other forms of colonial domination, nor...the right of these peoples to struggle to this end and to seek and receive support." Both the United States and Israel had to vote against that. They both understood that the phrase "colonial and racist regimes" referred to South Africa, which was a valued ally, while the ANC was one of the "more notorious terrorist groups" in the world. So obviously they didn't have a right to struggle against apartheid. And "foreign occupation or other forms of colonial domination" referred to the Israeli military occupation of the West Bank and Gaza, which was maintained precisely for the same reason it is now, by unilateral U.S. intervention.

The United States has been blocking a diplomatic settlement of the Israeli occupation for more than thirty years now. The process of preventing a diplomatic settlement has a name. It's called "the peace process." The peace process refers to whatever the United States happens to be doing, very often preventing political settlement, as in this case. And in this case, it's unilateral. It's not a pretty regime, it's harsh and brutal, and has been from the beginning. Still is. And therefore the United States and Israel had to vote against that qualification.

Well, that was 1988. Within a few years, the United States had been compelled to shift its position on South Africa. It had been compelled by popular action, including divestment campaigns, which didn't really affect the companies very much but had a big symbolic effect on undermining U.S. actions. There was technically an embargo, but U.S. trade with South Africa increased under the embargo, because they weren't paying any attention to it, for the reasons I just mentioned. But the popular campaign helped to shift the U.S. position. On the other case, Israel, popular efforts haven't yet shifted it, but they could. And in fact, there are proposals for divestment campaigns focused on U.S. aid to Israel. And on military weapons.

Now, you have to, of course, understand that when you talk about military producers, you're talking about virtually the whole high-tech economy. You can't pick out the military producers and leave the rest. In fact, if you look at government spending, you'll notice that in the last couple of years spending on the biology-based areas has been rapidly increasing. There's a reason for that. Every senator and person in Congress, no matter how right-wing they are—in fact the right-wingers know it better than the rest—understands that the way the economy works is you have to have a dynamic state sector in which the public assumes the costs and the risks, and if anything comes out, you put it into deep corporate pockets. That's what's called free enterprise, when you take an economics course. That's the way it works. And the cutting edge of the economy in the future is very likely to be the biology-based industries, biotech and genetic engineering and that kind of stuff. So therefore there has to be a lot more money going into basic biology and applications of it now, under the pretext of fighting bioterrorism.

You should see some of the things that are going on under that pretext. For example, the United States just destroyed the international effort, a six-year effort, to try to set up a verification procedure for an anti-bioterrorism treaty. The Clinton administration was opposed to it, primarily because it did not protect U.S. commercial interests, that is, the interests of U.S. pharmaceutical and biotech companies, since a verification system might look into what they're up to.

So the Clinton administration was opposed, but the Bush administration has killed it. Period. There were a number of reasons. One I just mentioned. But there were others. It turns out that the United States may be violating the treaties that already exist against bioterrorism. One of the ways it's reported to be doing this is by genetic engineering. Apparently, there is an effort to genetically engineer vaccine-resistant anthrax strains. That's considered a nightmare scenario among microbiologists: to create strains that are resistant to any vaccine or treatment. That's always been assumed to have been banned, but apparently the United States has been doing it, and there are a couple of other similar projects. And that's going to go on under the pretext of protection against bioterrorism.

But the main thing that will go on is developing the science and technology that will allow the biology-based industries of the future to be dominated by the United States. So, when you talk about going after weapons producers, it's a very broad category.

Maybe we could pick out representative companies, four or five, from each of the major sectors.

You're right. I mean, it has to be understood that these are symbolic gestures, which doesn't make them unimportant. They're symbolic, but extremely important. And they can be important if used as an educational and organizing device. That's very important. So, we should have no illusions that you're going to shut down weapons production, obviously not, that would mean shutting down the economy. But this effort is very important, just like in the South African case, because it's a way of organizing and educating, and it can have big effects. Within a couple of years, people shifted U.S. policy on South Africa.

The United States in the World

Excerpts from a question-and-answer session sponsored by the Students for Justice in Palestine, at the University of California–Berkeley on March 19, 2002.

Q: The next question is a popular one: How do you explain the recent shift in U.S. policy to support Palestine and the possible creation of a Palestinian state?

CHOMSKY: I explain it the same way I explain the U.S. shift in policy to dismantle the military system and hand it over to Andorra. Since it didn't happen, there is nothing to explain. There is no shift in policy whatsoever. It is a total farce. What happened is that Dick Cheney is running around the Middle East trying to get support for the upcoming war against Iraq, which is very hard because nobody wants it. In fact, most people hate it.

One of the problems is the Israeli tanks in Ramallah. Remember, when you read Israeli tanks and Israeli helicopters, you should translate it in your mind as saying U.S. helicopters and U.S. tanks and U.S. planes, which are sent to Israel with the certain knowledge that they are going to be used for this purpose. They happen to be flown by Israeli pilots, but it is us again in the case of the tanks, subsidizing their manufacture substantially; in the case of the helicopters, manufacturing them.

These are in effect U.S. military forces. Israel is like an offshore U.S. military base at this point. And the actions that it takes are actions that the U.S. authorizes or encourages. If they go one millimeter beyond what the United States wants, a quiet voice from Washington says, "That's it," and they quit. We just saw it again, a couple of days ago, when that soft voice came from Washington and said, Pull out the tanks and armed forces from the Palestinian cities, because it is screwing up Dick Cheney's mission. Instantly they withdrew. Instantly. Because that is the way it works in the mafia. If the don gives you orders, the guy down below doesn't kid around.

It has happened over and over. So when people talk about Israeli atrocities or Turkish atrocities, they should be saying U.S. atrocities, because that is where it is coming from. The same in Colombia.

So the shift on Palestine has been that the United States asked Israel to terminate the worst atrocities during the period of Cheney's visit because it was messing up his mission. There has been a lot of excitement about the fact that the United States sponsored a resolution on Israel in the UN Security Council, for the first time in twenty-five years. There has been less attention to what that resolution said.

What the resolution said was that the world has a vision of two states in the region, Israel and some Palestinian state, maybe off in Saudi Arabia in the desert somewhere, and it is a vision for the future. What that means is that that resolution does not even reach the level of South Africa during the worst days of apartheid.

During the darkest days of apartheid, forty years ago, South Africa not only had a "vision" of black states, it established them and, in fact, poured resources into them. Because it was hoping they would develop enough that the world would recognize them. That was the worst period of apartheid, in the early 1960s. And the vision that the United States is now offering to the world doesn't even reach that level. So we are supposed to be excited about it, but that is because we are supposed to be singing hosanna to our leaders no matter what they do. It is, again, part of a good education.

But what the United States has been doing, in fact, is undermining a diplomatic settlement. It still maintains its unilateral opposition to any diplomatic settlement, and this has been going on for twenty-five years. President after president of the United States has been alone in blocking a very broad international consensus on a political settlement that includes just about everybody, and the United States continues to block it today. Furthermore, the U.S. government is still refusing to allow even the most elementary measures to reduce the level of violence.

This is from the Afghan Student Union. What are the goals of the United States in Afghanistan with regard to the selection and preservation of the new government?

Like all of these questions about what the United States will do, that is something for us to decide. The new government, as the Afghan Student Union surely knows, was selected by the United States. Maybe it was a good choice, maybe not. But Hamid Karzai was the U.S. candidate, in fact, forced on everyone whether they wanted him or not.

In my opinion, the United States and Russia ought to do more: they shouldn't be giving aid to Afghanistan, they should be paying reparations.

These are the two countries that destroyed Afghanistan in the last twenty years, devastated it, and when you do that you should pay reparations. You don't give aid. And you try the people responsible for their crimes. So that is what ought to be happening. Of course, it won't happen. What we can, at most, hope for is that they will do something to try to repair the devastation that they have caused.

Unfortunately, they will do it for their own cynical reasons; unless we can pressure the U.S. government, nothing more hopeful will happen. There are sectors in the United States who think the United States should not even do that. So, for example, the *New Republic,* which is considered the leading journal of American liberalism. Their editorial position is that the United States should simply crush Afghanistan and leave it in ruins; and we should overcome our "obsession with nation-building" (November 5, 2001).

Once Afghanistan is no longer a problem for us, we will just leave it in ruins and go somewhere else. Well, that is one kind of voice of liberal intellectuals. But others don't quite rise to that level, and they think we ought to do something. But what will the United States do? With all of these questions, it depends on the pressures from the inside. None of these things are graven in stone. It depends on what people do.

A visiting scholar from Hungary asks, Don't you think that you greatly simplify all matters, as if the United States acts everywhere as an evil empire?

Do I simplify all matters by saying that "the United States acts everywhere as an evil empire"? Yes, that would certainly oversimplify things. And that is why I pointed out that the United States is behaving like every other power. The United States happens to be more powerful, so therefore it is, as you would expect, more violent. But, yes, everyone else is about the same. So when the British were running the world, they were doing the same thing.

Let's just take the Kurds. What was Britain doing about the Kurds? Here is a little lesson in history that they don't teach in the schools in England. But we know it from declassified documents. Britain had been the world dominant power, but by the time of the First World War, it was weakened by the war. After the war, if you look at the internal secret documents, the British were considering how they were going to continue to run Asia, now that they didn't have the military force to actually occupy it.

The suggestion was that they should turn to air power. Air power was just coming along at that time at the end of the First World War. So the idea was to use air power to attack civilians. They figured that would be a good way to reduce the costs of crushing the barbarians. Winston Churchill, who was then the colonial secretary, didn't think that was enough. He got a request from the

Royal Air Force office in Cairo asking him for permission, I am quoting it now, to use poison gas "against recalcitrant Arabs."

The recalcitrant Arabs they were talking about happened to be Kurds and Afghans, not Arabs. But, you know, by racist standards, anybody you want to kill is an Arab. So the question was, Should we use poison gas? And you have to remember, this is the First World War. Poison gas was the ultimate atrocity at that time. It was the worst thing you could imagine.

Well, this document was circulated around the British empire. The India office was resistant. They said, If you use poison gas against Kurds and Afghans, it is going to cause us problems in India, where we are having plenty of problems. There would be uprisings, and the people would be furious, and so on. They're not going to mind in England, of course, but in India they might. Churchill was outraged by this. And he said:

> I do not understand this squeamishness about the use of gas…. I am strongly in favour of using poisoned gas against uncivilised tribes…. It is not necessary to use only the most deadly gasses; gasses can be used which cause great inconvenience and would spread a lively terror and yet would leave no serious permanent effects on most of those affected…. [W]e cannot in any circumstances acquiesce in the non-utilisation of any weapons which are available to procure a speedy termination of the disorder which prevails on the frontier.

It will save British lives. We will use every
means that science permits us.

So that is the way you deal with Kurds and Afghans
when you are the British. What happened afterwards?
Well, we don't really know exactly. And the reason we
don't know exactly is that ten years ago the British government instituted what it called an Open Government
Policy to make government operations more transparent,
you know, to move toward democracy. So people will figure out what their government is doing.

And the first act of the Open Government Policy was to
remove from the Public Records Office—and, presumably,
destroy—all documents having to do with the use of poison gas and air power against the recalcitrant Arabs, that
is, the Kurds and Afghans. So we can be happy that we will
never have to know exactly what the outcome of this little Churchillian exercise was.

The British did succeed. There were a lot of disarma-
ment treaties at that time. In those years after the end of
the First World War, there were efforts to reduce war and
so on. The British succeeded in undermining every attempt
to bar the use of air power against civilians. And great
British statesmen were very pleased about this. Again, in
the internal record, the famous and greatly honored states-
man Lloyd George praised the government in 1932 for having, once again, blocked any barrier to the use of air power.

He said, "[W]e insisted on reserving the right to bomb
niggers." Yes, that is correct. So that is Britain, the other
major democracy.

If we run through the rest of the countries, we are going to find the same thing. So it would be surely a mistake to describe the United States as the evil empire. It just happens to be the most powerful force in the world since 1945.

And in the regions within its reach, even earlier, it wasn't very pretty. After all, there is a reason why we are talking here, in California. There used to be people who lived here, lots of people. Somehow they aren't around. Well it wasn't because, you know, they were given candy. You know why they aren't here. And you know why the U.S. border with Mexico is where it is. The United States conquered half of Mexico. And you know why a couple of hundred thousand Filipinos were killed a century ago, when we "Christianized" and "civilized" the Philippines. I won't go into what was going on in the Caribbean.

And so, even before the United States became the greatest power in the world, its record was like that of other powers. And we can talk about the Belgians or the Germans or the French. The French were committed, in the words of the Minister of War, to "exterminat[ing] the indigenous population" of Algeria. That was part of their civilizing and Christianizing mission. And so it goes.

So, yes, it would be a mistake to call the United States the evil empire, which is why I never do it.

How do you see U.S. intervention in the former Yugoslavia? Was it another form of U.S. imperialism or was it humanitarian intervention and justified?

Well, it is a long story. U.S. policy changed all over the place. At the beginning, the United States was the firmest backer of the unified Yugoslavia. That was its policy about ten years ago. When Slovenia and Croatia pulled out of the Yugoslav federation in 1991, they were quickly recognized by Germany, which was reasserting its own interest in the region, and recognized in a way that didn't pay any attention to the rights of the minority Serb population, which was a guarantee of a disaster. But the United States was first opposed to that.

Finally, as the great powers played their various games, the United States decided to pick Bosnia as its piece in the chess game. It blocked a peace settlement that might have worked, the Vance-Owen plan, developed by the former U.S. Secretary of State Cyrus Vance and David Owen from Britain. It had plenty of problems, but if you take a look at the plan, it is not very different from the way things ended up after years of slaughter.

The United States pressured the Bosnian government, then its chess piece, not to accept the plan. Predictably, this led to huge atrocities in the next couple of years. Finally, the United States stepped in and—you know the rest of the story—imposed the Dayton agreement in 1995. I don't see how you call any of this humanitarian. You can decide if the particular moves were right or wrong. But the humanitarian elements were nonexistent. With regard to Kosovo, even less so. We have a very rich record. There is a huge literature on the bombing of Kosovo.

There are some very interesting features of it. For one thing it is all extremely enthusiastic about a "new era in human history," an era of "humanitarian intervention," and so on. That is one feature, a lot of self-adulation.

Another feature is that it studiously ignores the very rich documentary record we have from the State Department, NATO, the Europeans, the Organization for Security and Cooperation in Europe, the Kosovo Verification Mission monitors, the UN, and the governments involved. There is an extremely rich record from them, from the West, on what was actually going on.

This is completely ignored in the literature. Have a look. As far as I know, my own books *New Military Humanism* and in more detail *A New Generation Draws the Line* are the only ones that even review it. My books did run through the record, and it is very rich. And here is what the record says. The record says that it was a pretty ugly place, no question. Nothing like Turkey, but pretty ugly. The most hawkish member of the Western coalition was Britain. They were the ones who were really gung ho about going ahead.

By January 1999, that is, two months before the bombing, the British government attributed most of the atrocities to the guerrillas, the Kosovo Liberation Army (KLA), which they described, just as the NATO documentation did, as coming across the border to carry out atrocities against the Serbs, in order to elicit a disproportionate response from the Serbs, which they could use to stir up support in the West. That was the position of the British government.

That was incidentally at the time of the Racak massacre, which is, according to the doctrine, what shifted Western opinion. The British were still saying most of the atrocities were attributed to the KLA, which they, like the

United States, called a terrorist force. We know from the rest of the record that nothing changed substantially in the next two months. Take a look at the State Department documentation and so on. Essentially nothing changed in the next two months. Until the time of the withdrawal of the monitors in preparation for the bombing.

After the bombing began, atrocities picked up enormously. If you take a look at the trial now taking place in the Hague, you will notice that the atrocities under consideration are for the period after the bombing. Once the bombing began and there was an invasion threat, then you started getting expulsions, atrocities, all sorts of things. Not before. The talk about returning the refugees to their homes as a great achievement overlooks the fact that the refugees were driven out after the bombing. Whatever you think about returning them to their homes, it is hardly a humanitarian effort.

Those are the facts, and I won't go on. Whatever it was, again, you can think it was good or bad, but there was no humanitarian element. Zero. It had some other purpose.

In recent months, mainstream news sources like CNN, the San Francisco Chronicle, et cetera, are starting to discuss the Israel oppression and genocide in Iraq via the sanctions. Do you think 9-11 has started the initial cracking of the mainstream media?

I don't watch CNN, so I can't say. I was subjected to CNN for a month, I have to admit, in November 2001. My wife and I were in India, where it is very hard to get international newspapers. We had to watch CNN, that torture, every night. But I didn't notice what you're describing. Since I don't watch it generally, I can't say. It just looked like patriotic drivel to me. But from what I read, which is the print press, I don't see that change. I don't see any discussion of the effect of the sanctions or of Israeli policy, except when it is beginning to interfere with what the United States is doing.

So there was objection to the recent acts that were interfering with Cheney's mission. There was objection to that. Meanwhile, the atrocities escalate with the U.S. support. The United States continues to provide military and diplomatic support. It continues to prevent a diplomatic settlement, just as went on under Clinton. I mentioned the UN resolutions. There are even worse cases.

Let me mention another. The Geneva Conventions, as you should know, were established right after the Second World War to formally criminalize the atrocities of the Nazis. That is the Geneva Conventions. There are high-contracting parties of the Geneva Conventions, including the United States, which are obligated by the most solemn treaties to enforce the Geneva Conventions. That's their responsibility.

If the United States doesn't enforce it, that is a crime. The Fourth Geneva Convention applies to territories under military occupation. Does it apply to the Israeli occupied territories? Here there is a split in the world. The entire world says yes. Israel says no. And the United States abstains, since Clinton. Before that it adopted the virtually unanimous position in the world. It abstains because it doesn't want to come out against a core principle of international law, particularly given the circumstances in which it was enacted, namely, to criminalize Nazi crimes. So the United States abstains. U.S. abstention kills it, which means that it doesn't get reported. It falls out of history, but it's there.

For example, in October 2000, right after the second intifada started, the Security Council, once again, voted that the Geneva Conventions apply to the Israeli occupied territories. The vote was fourteen to zero. The United States abstained. That makes it customary international law. The Geneva Conventions make illegal just about everything the United States and Israel are doing in the occupied territories. Settlements, troops, it's all illegal. That's the actual policy. The shift that people think they're seeing is an illusion, in my opinion. This is the actual policy, and until that policy is changed, it's going to go on.

How and why do you think the media represented Muslims the way they did after the September 11 attack?

Actually, it was better than I had expected. There was an attempt, probably sincere, to distinguish the atrocities from Muslims in general, to a considerable extent. You've got to give credit where credit is due. They did not stigmatize Muslims the way they might have. There is plenty of anti-Arab racism in the United States and anti-Muslim racism. It's kind of the last legitimate form of racism, legitimate in the sense that you don't have to deny it.

But I don't think it notably increased after September 11. In fact, there were efforts to dampen it down.

President Bush recently named Iran as one of the countries of the "axis of evil." He has also threatened military action. How real is the attack on Iran?

The phrase "axis of evil" that Bush's speechwriters came up with, "evil"; obviously, if you want to scare people, you talk about evil. "Axis" is supposed to call up memories of the Nazis and so on. Actually, this is certainly no axis. Iran and Iraq have been at war for twenty years. North Korea has less to do with either of them than France does. So that's not an axis. North Korea was probably tossed in, for one thing, because it is an easy target. If you feel like bombing it, nobody's going to care. Also, because it's not Muslim. So it kind of deflects the idea that you are after the Muslims. So we'll put North Korea aside.

What about Iran? Well, take a look at the history. Iran has sometimes been "evil" and sometimes been "good" over the last fifty years. If you look at the trajectory, you get the answer to your question. In 1953, Iran was evil, the epitome of evil. Why? Because it had a conservative nationalist elected government that was trying to take control of its own resources, which had been run by the British up until then. So it was the epitome of evil. The government had to be overthrown by a military coup carried out by the United States and Britain. The Shah was reinstalled.

Then for the next twenty-six years it was good. The Shah compiled one of the worst human rights records in the world. If you read Amnesty International reports, he's ranked highest. But he was serving U.S. interests. He captured Saudi Arabian islands, helping to control the region and supporting the United States on everything. And he was good. So you read the press, there was no commentary on any Iranian crimes. President Carter particularly admired the Shah. Just a couple of months before he was overthrown, he said how impressed he was by the Shah's "progressive administration," and so on.

In 1979, Iran became evil again. They pulled out of the imperial system. And since then they have been evil. They haven't been following orders. Actually, it is an interesting situation. Here is a case where a really powerful lobby, the oil lobby in the United States—the energy companies—want to reintegrate Iran into the world system, but the government won't allow it. They want Iran to be an enemy.

One of the things this "axis of evil" business did was undermine the reformist elements in Iran, which have the majority of the population behind them, and give a shot in the arm to the most reactionary clerical elements. But all of this is considered okay, and we have to ask why.

My suspicion—this is speculation, because we don't have the documentary record—is that the reason is the usual one. It's called "establishing credibility." Any mafia don will explain it to you. If somebody gets out of line, they have to be punished. Others have to understand that that's not tolerable behavior. That was the main official reason for the bombing of Serbia and Kosovo, "establishing NATO credibility." You don't step out of line. You follow orders, or else.

My guess is that's the main motive for the current policy. I don't think the United States is going to attack Iran. It would be too dangerous and costly, but if the more reactionary clerical elements maintain power, that keeps Iran from being integrated into the international system.

There presumably will be an attack against Iraq, which is a very tricky operation to plan. The reasons for the invasion of Iraq, you can be absolutely certain, have nothing to do with the official statements. That is not even a question. It is another service of the educated classes that they manage to keep this quiet. They all know, of course.

When you read George Bush, Tony Blair, Bill Clinton, or all the rest of them, they tell you, "We have to go after Saddam Hussein, this guy is such an evil monster that he even used chemical weapons against his own people. And how can we let someone like that survive?"

It is true. He used chemical weapons against his own people, but there is a phrase missing: "with the aid and support of Daddy Bush," who thought that was just fine. He continued to provide aid and support for the monster, and so did Britain. Long after the worst atrocities that Saddam carried out, including the gassing of the Kurds and the rest, the United States and Britain happily gave him aid and support, including aid that enabled him to develop weapons of mass destruction, as they knew perfectly well.

At that time he was far more dangerous than he is today. Iraq was then a much more powerful state. And nothing was considered wrong with this. In fact, in early 1990—a couple of months before the invasion of Kuwait—President Bush Number One sent a high-level senatorial delegation headed by Bob Dole, later the Republican presidential candidate, to Iraq to convey his greetings to his friend Saddam Hussein. They told him how much Bush appreciated his great contributions, and that he should disregard critical comments he is hearing occasionally from the American press.

We have this free press thing here and every once in a while somebody gets out of line, and maybe one of five thousand correspondents has a few remarks about how Saddam Hussein committed crimes, but he was informed to just forget about that. He was also told that a critical commentator on Voice of America would be removed so he wouldn't have that unpleasant experience of hearing about the bad things that he does. And that was a couple of months before he became the "Beast of Baghdad" and was conquering the world and so on and so forth.

We know his crimes are not the reason for the intended conquest. Nor is it his development of weapons of mass destruction.

If those aren't the reasons, what are the reasons? Well, the reasons are pretty obvious. Iraq has the second-largest oil reserves in the world after Saudi Arabia. It has been obvious all along that one way or another the United States would do something to regain control over that immense resource, which is much larger than the reserves near under the Caspian Sea. Certainly the United States is going to deny those resources to its adversaries. Right now France and Russia have the inside track on them and the United States is looking to take it over.

The question is how. It is a very tricky operation. There are a lot of technical problems like, you know, exactly how you do it. That is what is being discussed. But those are minor problems. The real problem is that a new regime must be imposed, and the new regime must be completely undemocratic.

There is a reason for that. If there is any element of democracy in the new regime, the population will have some voice in what is happening. That is what democracy is. The population gets maybe a minimal voice. But the problem is that the majority of the population is Shiite, which means that to the extent that the majority of the population has any voice, it is going to move toward relations with Iran, which is the last thing the U.S. government wants. We could go into the reasons for that, but it is obvious that the United States doesn't want this. Furthermore, the Kurds in the northern part of Iraq, who are another big part of the population, are on a quest for some kind of autonomy, and Turkey will go berserk if that happens, as will the United States.

So somehow you have to have a regime change that restores something exactly like Saddam Hussein, a Sunni-based, military regime that will be able to control the population. Furthermore, this has been completely explicit. You may recall that in March 1991, right after the Gulf War, the United States had total control of the area. There was a Shiite rebellion in the south, a big rebellion, including rebelling Iraqi generals.

They didn't ask for any aid from the United States. The most they asked for was that the United States allow them access to captured Iraqi equipment. George Bush the First had a different idea. He authorized his friend Saddam Hussein to use air power to crush the Shiite resistance.

General Norman Schwarzkopf later said that when he authorized Saddam to use aircraft, he was misled by the Iraqis. He didn't realize that when he authorized them to use military aircraft, they were actually going to do it. So he was fooled. And this really shows how awful Hussein is. He tricks you all the time. So he used military aircraft to crush the Shiites and the Kurds in the north.

Right about that time, Thomas Friedman, who was then the diplomatic correspondent for the *New York Times*—"diplomatic correspondent" is a term that means State Department spokesman at the *New York Times*, and he was giving the State Department line—was pretty frank about it. He said the best of all worlds for the United States would be an "iron-fisted military junta" that would rule Iraq the same way Saddam Hussein did, but with a change of name, because Saddam Hussein was kind of embarrassing at that point. And if we can't get that, we will have to do with second best. But that would be the best of all worlds and that is the world they are trying to find now. That is why the CIA and the State Department are now organizing meetings of Iraqi generals who defected in the 1990s.

That is not going to be so simple to arrange, but that is perhaps what is being planned.

Part IV

The Obama Era

The U.S. Elections and Iraq

In March 2008 Stephen Shalom interviewed Noam Chomsky about the future of U.S. policy in the Middle East under a future, new presidential administration.

SHALOM: Eight long years of the George W. Bush administration are coming to an end. The next U.S. president may well be a Democrat. What difference would a Democratic administration make in U.S. policy toward the Middle East?

CHOMSKY: The short answer is that we do not really know and can only speculate. The reason has to do with the way elections are designed, a topic we discuss earlier in the book (see *Perilous Power*, pp. 47f.). Issues are typically marginalized, a reflection of the general elite distaste for democracy and fear of its consequences. The concern is heightened by the fact that on a host of major issues, both parties are to the right of the electorate, which tends to have consistent and coherent positions over time.[1]

The current electoral campaigns conform to the usual pattern, and therefore leave the stands of the candidates on crucial issues unclear. There has been a flow of largely vacuous rhetoric; favorites have been "change," "hope," "unity," "experience," and a few others. One can investigate the websites of the candidates, where there are some statements about plans. They are typically not very specific, and their significance is debatable: What matters more is what the candidates and campaign managers stress prominently and insistently, not words posted on Internet sites that can be variously interpreted or ignored at will. It is not unusual for candidates, once elected, even to back away from explicit and prominent campaign promises. Clinton, for example, "put the call for universal health care at the center of his program," Vicente Navarro recalls. "But, once president, his closeness to Wall Street and his intellectual dependence on Robert Rubin of Wall Street (who became his Secretary of the Treasury) made him leery of antagonizing the insurance industry," so he backed away from a program that has long been strongly favored by a large majority of the population.[2]

On "super-Tuesday" February 5, the day of many crucial primaries, the *Wall Street Journal* ran a lead story with the headline "Issues Recede in '08 Contest as Voters Focus on Character: Candidates Pitch Style, Avoid Big Ideas; 'Folks Are Tired of Partisan Paralysis.'" The story is largely correct, but not entirely. First, issues could hardly "recede" very far since they had been kept in the background to begin with. Second, while it may be that "voters focus on character," they are given little choice when "candidates pitch style, avoid big ideas." And while "folks" are no doubt irritated that the government does not serve their interests (as polls regularly show), that hardly indicates that they have abandoned those interests.[3]

The occasional departures from the pattern reveal a good deal about "really existing democracy," and also give some indication of what might lead to changes in Middle East policy. The most dramatic change from 2004 to 2008 has to do with health care, which for a long time has been a leading domestic concern of the public. Not surprisingly: Per capita expenditures are twice those of other industrial societies, and health outcomes are among the worst in the industrial world, barely above Third World standards in some respects. Forty-seven million people have no health coverage apart from emergency rooms, the most cruel (and expensive) form of guaranteed health care. A great many others have insufficient coverage, a leading cause of bankruptcy. Navarro observes that "nearly 40% of people in the U.S. who are dying because of terminal illness are *worrying about paying for care*—how their families are going to pay the medical bills, now and after they die. No other developed country comes close to these levels of insensitivity and inhumanity."[4]

The public has long favored a government health care system to overcome the huge administrative and marketing costs, intrusion into doctor-patient relations, profits, and other burdens of the privatized system. As discussed above (See *Perilous Power*, pp. 47–48), during the 2004 campaign Kerry could not mention any government involvement in health care, the press reported, because it was "politically impossible" and had "so little political support"—only the support of the large majority of the population, as in earlier years. In 2008, by contrast, government involvement does have "political support." Beginning with John Edwards, Democratic candidates have put forth proposals that partially approach what the public has been seeking for decades. What changed between 2004 and 2008? Not public opinion. Rather, a significant element of the functioning political system has become concerned about the health care catastrophe: the manufacturing industry. General Motors estimates that it costs over $1,000 more to produce a car in Detroit than in Windsor, Canada, right across the border, because of health care costs. Corporate distress was sufficient to shift policies from "politically impossible" to politically possible.

With regard to Middle East policy, unless there is some comparable shift among sectors of authentic power, it is unlikely that policies will change significantly—assuming, that is, that the public remains marginalized: "spectators" rather than "participants," in accord with prevailing democratic theory.

Nevertheless, some changes are likely. The Bush administration has been far to the radical nationalist and adventurist extreme of the policy spectrum, and has been subjected to unprecedented mainstream criticism for that reason. It is possible that McCain might be similar, but a Democratic candidate is likely to shift more toward the centrist norm. However, the spectrum is narrow. Thus the Bush National Security Strategy of September 2002 was harshly criticized right away, even in the major foreign policy journals, but more because of its brazen style and arrogance than because of its content, as was pointed out by Clinton's Secretary of State Madeleine Albright, who was surely aware of Clinton's fairly similar doctrine.

Looking at the records and statements of the candidates, I see little reason to expect significant changes in policy in the Middle East.

Take the issue of Iraq. It is important to bear in mind that neither Democratic candidate has expressed a principled objection to the invasion. By that I mean the kind of objection that was universally expressed when the Russians invaded Afghanistan or when Saddam Hussein invaded Kuwait: condemnation on the grounds that aggression is a crime—in fact, the "supreme international crime" differing from others in that it encompasses all the evil that follows, as the Nuremberg Tribunal determined. No one criticized those invasions merely as a "strategic blunder" or as involvement in "another country's civil war, a war [we] can't win" (Obama and Clinton, respectively, on the Iraq invasion).

Similarly, there was universal and principled condemnation of Russian criminal atrocities in Chechnya. The crime is not mitigated by the fact that Putin's brutal measures appear to have largely succeeded in restoring order and reconstruction under a Chechen government, with fighting "limited and sporadic" and Grozny in the midst of a "building boom" after having been reduced to rubble by the Russian attack.[5] No one applauds Putin for the grand achievement. The criticism of the Iraq war, in contrast, is on grounds of cost and failure; what are called "pragmatic reasons," a stance that is considered hard-headed, serious, moderate—in the case of Western crimes. If General Petraeus could approach Putin's achievements in Chechnya, he might be crowned king. For that reason alone a significant change of course is unlikely.

The intentions of the Bush administration, and presumably of McCain, were outlined in a Declaration of Principles released by the White House in November 2007—an agreement between Bush and the U.S.-backed Maliki government of Iraq, which is housed in the heavily protected U.S.-run Green Zone in Baghdad. The Declaration allows U.S. forces to remain in Iraq indefinitely to "deter foreign aggression" (though the only aggression threatened in the region is posed by the United States and Israel, presumably not the intention) and to maintain internal security—though not, of course, internal security for a government that would reject U.S. domination. The Declaration also commits Iraq to facilitate and encourage "the flow of foreign investments to Iraq, especially American investments." This unusually brazen expression of imperial will was underscored when Bush quietly issued yet another of his hundreds of "signing statements," declaring that he will reject crucial provisions of congressional legislation that he had just signed, including the provision that forbids spending taxpayer money "to establish any military installation or base for the purpose of providing for the permanent stationing of United States Armed Forces in Iraq" or "to exercise United States control of the oil resources of Iraq." Shortly before, the *New York Times* had reported that Washington "insists that the Baghdad government give the United States broad authority to conduct combat operations," a demand that "faces a potential buzz saw of opposition from Iraq, with its ... deep sensitivities about being seen as a dependent state."[6]

In brief, Iraq is to remain a client state, agreeing to allow permanent U.S. military installations (called "enduring" in the preferred Orwellism), granting the United States the right to conduct combat operations freely, and ensuring U.S.

investors priority in accessing its huge oil resources—a reasonably clear statement of the goals of the invasion that were evident to anyone not blinded by doctrine.*

What are the alternatives of the Democrats? They were clarified in March 2007, when the House and Senate approved Democratic proposals setting deadlines for withdrawal. The proposals were analyzed by General Kevin Ryan (ret.), senior fellow at Harvard University's Belfer Center of International Affairs.[7] He pointed out that the proposals permit the president to waive their restrictions in the interests of "national security," which leaves the door wide open. They permit troops to remain in Iraq "as long as they are performing one of three specific missions: protecting US facilities, citizens, or forces; combating Al Qaeda or international terrorists; and training Iraqi security forces." U.S. facilities include the huge U.S. military bases being built around the country and the U.S. Embassy—actually a self-contained city within a city, unlike any other embassy in the world. None of these major construction projects are under way with the expectation that they will be abandoned. If U.S. troops are in close contact with the Iraqi security forces, they may need plenty of protection, because a majority of Arab Iraqis regard them as a legitimate target of attack. Combating terrorism and training Iraqi military and police are also open-ended and highly flexible commitments. Ryan concludes that the proposals are likely to leave about as many troops as had been

---

*As noted on p. 198, these demands had to be abandoned in the face of strong Iraqi resistance, carrying forward the U.S. failure to impose its will since the invasion.

in Iraq for several years: "Military experts would rightfully point out that the bills before Congress are more correctly understood as a re-missioning of our troops." Ryan sums up: "Perhaps a good strategy—but not a withdrawal."

It is difficult to see much difference between the Democratic proposals of March 2007 and those of Obama and Clinton. Both of the candidates provide figures for planned troop withdrawal, but as Obama foreign policy advisor Samantha Power commented, these are tentative, a "best case scenario." Power was lambasted for speaking the truth (and later resigned from the campaign following impolite references to Clinton).[8]

The Obama-Clinton proposals not only leave open the continued use of mercenaries ("contractors"), who match U.S. forces in number, but also ignore the issue of logistics and supply, which require huge operations, often traveling from Kuwait through dangerous territory in southern Iraq. And they say nothing about continued bombing. Those who recall the last years of the Indochina wars will recognize that open door—for example, in rural Cambodia, where U.S. bombing exceeded the total bombing in all theaters of World War II and "drove an enraged populace into the arms of an insurgency [the Khmer Rouge] that had enjoyed relatively little support before the bombing began."[9] Current bombing levels are apparently substantial. James Paul of Global Policy Forum, who has followed the war closely, writes that "Balad Airbase, north of Baghdad, is probably the busiest air facility in the world. Now, some of that is supply shipments, but fundamentally, it's attacks—everything from drones to fixed wing [planes], all coming at an enormous cost of human life."[10]

The proposals are also silent about the more advanced forms of state terror available to high-tech outlaw states. Thus when Israeli forces murdered the quadriplegic cleric Sheikh Yassin as he was leaving a mosque in March 2004, along with seven civilians nearby, they appear to have used a helicopter-fired hellfire missile directed by a drone, one of many such cases.[11] The assassination of Yassin, a revered figure who was the spiritual leader of Hamas and considered to be one of its more conciliatory figures, set off massive protests in Iraq and the murder of four U.S. contractors in Fallujah by the previously unknown "Brigades of Martyr Ahmed Yassin," then a murderous reaction by U.S. Marines killing hundreds of people that contributed to a sudden spread of violence throughout much of Iraq, barely contained.

The United States has a much longer reach. In one recent case, "on Oct. 30, 2006, a Hellfire missile hit a madressah in Bajaur killing ... 80–85 people, mostly students. Even if those killed were allegedly training to become Al Qaeda militants, and even if a few key Al Qaeda leaders such as Abu Laith al-Libi have been eliminated, the more usual outcome has been flattened houses, dead and maimed children, and a growing local population that seeks revenge against Pakistan and the U.S."[12]

This terrorist incident was hailed as a grand achievement of the "war on terror" because Libi, the presumed target, was "believed to have plotted and executed attacks against U.S. and coalition forces." The 80–85 students, dead and maimed children, and other "collateral damage" passed unnoticed. Other terrorist atrocities are treated quite differently, and not all are permitted to celebrate them. There was, for example, very prominent and vivid coverage of the murder of eight students in the Merkaz HaRav seminary in Jerusalem, the spiritual center of the settler movement, and great outrage over Palestinian support for the atrocity, even though Palestinian endorsement of violence can be attributed to "recent actions by Israel, especially attacks on Gaza that killed nearly 130 people, an undercover operation in Bethlehem that killed four militants and the announced expansion of several West Bank settlements, [which] have led to despair and rage among average Palestinians who thirst for revenge." Similarly, those who denounce Palestinians for heartlessly celebrating deaths of Jews did not seem to mind when "angry students and local residents lined up behind police tapes, chanting, 'Death to Arabs.'"[13]

Overall, it is not easy to find substantial grounds for expecting significant changes in U.S. policy with regard to Iraq with Democrats in the White House and Congress, though it is likely that there would be a softening of the extremist Bush-Cheney (and probably McCain) stance.

Iran

SHALOM: What about the issue of Iran? Is there reason to expect a different U.S. policy if a Democrat wins the election?

CHOMSKY: Obama is considered the more moderate of the two remaining candidates, and his leading slogan is "change." So let us keep to him.

With regard to Iran, Obama calls for more willingness to negotiate, but within the standard doctrinal constraints. His reported position is that he "would offer economic inducements and a possible promise not to seek 'regime change' if Iran stopped meddling in Iraq and cooperated on terrorism and nuclear issues," and stopped "acting irresponsibly" by supporting Shiite militant groups in Iraq.[14]

Some obvious questions come to mind. For example, how would we react if Ahmadinejad said he would offer a possible promise not to seek "regime change" in Israel if it stopped its illegal activities in the occupied territories and cooperated on terrorism and nuclear issues? Or if, in the 1980s, the Kremlin had announced that it might not seek "regime change" in Pakistan (or Saudi Arabia, or the United States) if it stopped "acting irresponsibly" by supporting terrorists in Afghanistan, then under Russian occupation? If the comparisons sound outlandish, that tells us a lot about the reigning doctrinal system.

It is noteworthy that Obama's moderate approach is well to the militant side of public opinion—a fact that passes unnoticed, as is often the case. Like all other viable candidates, Obama has insisted throughout the electoral campaign that the United States must threaten Iran with attack (the standard phrase is "Keep all options open")—a violation of the UN Charter, if anyone cares. But a large majority of Americans have disagreed: 75 percent favor building better relations with Iran, as compared with 22 percent who favor "implied threats."[15] All the surviving candidates, then, are opposed by three-fourths of the public on this issue.

That is not unusual. I have already mentioned a leading domestic issue, health care. To take a case with some similarity to Iran, two-thirds of Americans favor establishing diplomatic relations with Cuba, as has largely been true since polls began to be taken thirty years ago. But as in the past, all candidates reject that option and insist that the United States must continue its efforts to strangle Cuba economically, in splendid isolation, supported only by Israel (which votes with the United States reflexively but violates the U.S. sanctions) and an occasional Pacific island. In this regard, too, Obama is considered the most moderate of the candidates, "hinting that he might be open to changes in US policy if Havana made moves towards openness and democracy"[16]—a stand that might seem forthcoming to a Martian observer who knows nothing about Washington's record, past and present, with regard to tyrannical regimes. Even much of the business world favors entering into normal relations with Cuba. But the state interest in punishing Cubans for "successful defiance" of the master prevails. The disgraceful record of almost a half-century of terror and economic strangulation carries lessons for U.S.-Iran policy today: Iranians must be punished for overthrowing the tyrant whom the United States and Britain imposed when they destroyed Iranian parliamentary democracy in 1953 (to great acclaim in the national press).

In many respects, the conduct of international affairs resembles the Mafia. The Godfather does not tolerate disobedience, even from a small storekeeper who fails to pay protection money. "The rot might spread," as leading statesmen have warned, and the system of control might unravel.

Like the other candidates, Obama is far to the right of the public on resolution of the confrontation with Iran, a matter of no slight importance: British military historian Correlli Barnett hardly exaggerates when he warns that an attack on Iran by the United States (or its Israeli client) "would effectively launch World War III."[17]

American and Iranian opinion on the core issue of nuclear policy has been carefully studied. In both the United States and Iran, a large majority holds that the latter should have the rights of any signer of the Non-Proliferation Treaty: to develop nuclear power but not nuclear weapons. The same large majorities favor establishing a "nuclear-weapons-free zone in the Middle East that would include both Islamic countries and Israel." Over 80 percent of Americans favor eliminating nuclear weapons altogether— a legal obligation of the states with nuclear weapons, officially rejected by the Bush administration. And surely Iranians agree with Americans that Washington should end its military threats and turn toward normal relations. At a forum in Washington when the polls were released in January 2007, Joseph Cirincione, senior vice president for National Security and International Policy at the Center for American Progress (and Obama advisor), said the polls showed "the common sense of both the American people and the Iranian people, [who] seem to be able to rise above the rhetoric of their own leaders to find common sense solutions to some of the most crucial questions" facing the two nations, favoring pragmatic diplomatic solutions to their differences.[18] Establishing a nuclear-weapons-free zone would be particularly important, even apart from the fact that the United States and Britain have a unique commitment to this objective. In their effort to concoct a thin legal justification for their invasion of Iraq, they charged that Iraq was in violation of UN Security Council Resolution 687, which requires Iraq to eliminate weapons of mass destruction. The fate of that charge is well known, but few recall Article 14 of Resolution 687, which affirms "the goal of establishing in the Middle East a zone free from weapons of mass destruction and all missiles for their delivery and the objective of a global ban on chemical weapons," and thus surely commits the initiators and supporters of the resolution to that goal: crucially, the states that appealed to the resolution to justify their aggression.

The polls suggest that if the United States and Iran were functioning democratic societies, in which public opinion was a significant factor in determining policy on crucial issues, the very dangerous U.S.-Iran confrontation might be resolved peaceably. The prospects, however, seem remote. The opinions of the American public are so far beyond what is "politically possible" that these important polls do not even seem to have been reported. They clearly do not enter into the electoral process or discussion in the media and journals. Sophisticates commonly argue that policy cannot be "poll-driven." The premier polling agency, the Program on International Policy Attitudes at the University of Maryland, reports that "[w]hen ABC News correspondent Martha Raddatz cited polling data showing majority opposition to the Iraq war, [Dick] Cheney responded, 'So?' Asked, 'So—you don't care what the American people think?' he responded, 'No,' and explained, 'I think you cannot be blown off course by the fluctuations in the public opinion polls.'" As she attempted to explain Cheney's comments, White House spokeswoman Dana Perino was asked whether the public should have "input." Her reply was: "You had your input. The American people have input every four years, and that's the way our system is set up."[19]

Correct. Every four years the American people can choose between candidates whose views they reject, and then they should shut up.

Evidently failing to understand democratic theory, the public strongly disagrees. "Eighty-one percent say when making 'an important decision' government leaders 'should pay attention to public opinion polls because this will help them get a sense of the public's views.'" And when asked "whether they think that 'elections are the only time when the views of the people should have influence, or that also between elections leaders should consider the views of the people as they make decisions,' an extraordinary 94 percent say that government leaders should pay attention to the views of the public between elections."[20]

Once again, however, the views of the public "lack political support" and hence can be ignored.

Nevertheless, circumstances may change. Public opinion may not remain marginalized and easily ignored. The concentrations of domestic economic power that largely shape policy may come to recognize that their interests are better served by joining the general public, and the rest of the world, than by accepting Washington's hard line. Though we do not have internal records, there is good reason to believe that the Pentagon is opposed to an attack on Iran. The March 11 resignation of Admiral William Fallon as head of the Central Command, responsible for the Middle East, was widely interpreted as tracing back to his opposition to an attack, probably shared with the military command generally. The December 2007 National Intelligence Estimate (NIE) reporting that Iran had not pursued a nuclear weapons program since 2003, when it sought and failed to reach a comprehensive settlement with the United States (See *Perilous Power*, p. 232), perhaps reflects opposition of the intelligence community to military action.[21]

Israel is a rare exception to global opposition to a U.S. attack on Iran. Israel has long wanted the United States to eliminate the only power in the region it cannot dominate on its own. However, it is also possible, as Trita Parsi has argued, that Israel might come to realize that it could gain from reestablishing its traditional close relations with Iran, continuing through the 1980s after Khomeini took power—a relationship so close that Israel and its U.S. lobby "lobbied the United States *not* to pay attention to Iranian rhetoric" about Israel's destruction.[22]

There are many uncertainties, and one should not underestimate Bush-Cheney adventurism, desperation, and dedication to violence, which would render all speculation moot. But it is hard to see concrete signs that a Democratic presidency would improve the situation very much, let alone bring policy into line with American or world opinion.

Israel–Palestine and the United States

SHALOM: And what about the issue of Israel-Palestine? What differences in policy can we expect here as a result of the forthcoming U.S. election?

CHOMSKY: On Israel-Palestine too, the candidates have provided no reason to expect any constructive change. Keeping again to Obama, the candidate of "change" and "hope," his website states that he "strongly supports the U.S.-Israel relationship, believes that our first and incontrovertible commitment in the Middle East must be to the security of Israel, America's strongest ally in the Middle East." He may have meant "closest ally," but taking the words literally, Israel is indeed the "strongest ally." Transparently, it is the Palestinians who face by far the most severe security problem—in fact, a problem of survival. But the Palestinians are not a "strong ally." At most, they might be a very weak one. Hence their plight merits little concern, in accord with the operative principle that human rights are largely determined by contributions to power, profit, and doctrinal needs.

Obama's website presents him as a superhawk on Israel. "He believes that Israel's right to exist as a Jewish state should never be challenged." He is not on record as demanding that the right of countries to exist as Muslim (Christian, White) states "should never be challenged." During the 2006 Lebanon war, "Obama stood up strongly for Israel's right to defend itself from Hezbollah raids and rocket attacks," but had nothing to say about Lebanon's right to defend itself from the U.S.-backed Israeli aggression that killed over 1,000 people and destroyed much of the country. He "is an original cosponsor of the Senate resolution expressing support for Israel [during its invasion of Lebanon], condemning the [Hezbollah] attacks, and calling for strong action against Iran and Syria," though vastly greater U.S. support for the aggressors is apparently right and just, just as it was during Israel's four previous invasions of Lebanon since 1978. "Throughout the war, Barack Obama made clear that Israel should not be pressured into a cease-fire that did not deal with the threat of Hezbollah missiles." Rather, Israel must be permitted to destroy Lebanese civilian society until it is free from the threat of a deterrent to its assaults: No missiles attributed to Hezbollah had struck Israel after its withdrawal from Lebanon in 2000, until the July 2006 war.

Obama calls for increasing foreign aid "to ensure that [the] funding priorities [for military and economic assistance to Israel] are met." He also insists forcefully that the United States must not "recognize Hamas unless it renounced its fundamental mission to eliminate Israel." No state can recognize Hamas, a political party, so what he must be referring to is the government formed by Hamas after a free election that came out "the wrong way" and is therefore illegitimate, in accord with prevailing elite concepts of "democracy." To leave no ambiguity, Obama's website explains that he was "a cosponsor of the Palestinian Anti-Terrorism Act of 2006. Introduced in the wake of Hamas' victory in the Palestinian elections, this act outlaws direct assistance to any entity of the Palestinian Authority controlled by Hamas." Punishment of the Palestinians for voting the wrong way must continue, Obama holds, until Hamas meets the three conventional conditions: "recognize Israel, abandon violence, and abide by previous agreements made between the Palestinian Authority and Israel."

Obama does not ignore Palestinians: "Obama believes that a better life for Palestinian families is good for both

Israelis and Palestinians." He also adds a vacuous statement about two states living side by side, leaving it in a form that has been acceptable to Israel ever since the Israeli ultraright considered a meaningless version of a two-state settlement in 1996, followed in this a few years later by the more dovish parties (See *Perilous Power*, pp. 171f.).

Also conventional is Obama's failure to mention that the United States and Israel continue to reject for themselves the very conditions they have imposed on Hamas: Obviously they do not recognize Palestine or renounce violence, and though the facts are evaded, they also reject previous commitments, including the "Road Map" (See *Perilous Power*, p. 240).

Virtually every reference to Hamas identifies it as the Iranian-backed group dedicated to the destruction of Israel as its "fundamental mission." One will search in vain for condemnation of the official Israeli-American commitment to destroy Palestine (the 1989 Shamir-Peres-Baker Plan), a fundamental mission that was not mere words: Shamir, Peres, and Baker were actively implementing that commitment at the time of their 1989 declaration, as before (See *Perilous Power*, pp. 169f.), and their successors continue to do so today, with only rhetorical change. It is irrelevant that Hamas has repeatedly proposed (and unilaterally implemented) a cease-fire to allow negotiations to proceed toward the political settlement approved by the international consensus that the United States and Israel have unilaterally rejected. Similarly, it is irrelevant that Hamas has repeatedly advocated a two-state settlement in terms of this consensus, as when Hamas Prime Minister Ismail Haniyeh called for "statehood for the West Bank and Gaza" or when the most militant Hamas leader Khalid Mish'al, in exile in Damascus, called for "the establishment of a truly sovereign and independent Palestinian state on the territories occupied by Israel in June 1967."[23]

Such facts cannot be facts, virtually by definition, because they conflict with deeply held doctrine. Accordingly, though staring us in the face, they are invisible, as is the U.S.-Israeli leadership of the rejectionist camp tracing back to 1971 and 1976 (See *Perilous Power*, pp. 166–169). It must be that the United States is an "honest broker," not the leading barrier to political settlement. Facts cannot be permitted to interfere with such crucial doctrines of the faith.

Operative U.S.-Israeli policy conforms to the Olmert "convergence" program (See *Perilous Power*, pp. 238f.). The program was withdrawn after the Lebanon war as too forthcoming, but remains the basic guideline for policy. Always with U.S. backing, apart from some mild clucking of tongues, Israel is continuing to construct the Separation Wall, by now very clearly an annexation wall. The authoritative determination by the highest international legal authority (the International Court of Justice, commonly known as the World Court) that the Wall violates international law (See *Perilous Power*, pp. 173f.) has joined other unwanted historical facts in the memory hole, cavernous but brimful. It is of no concern that the Court ruled that all settlement activities violate the Geneva conventions, established to formally criminalize Nazi crimes. The Court ruled that "the Fourth Geneva Convention, and international human rights law are applicable to the Occupied Palestinian Territory and must there[fore] be faithfully complied with by Israel," so that populations cannot be transferred there, and the segments of the Separation Wall "being built by Israel to protect the settlements are ipso facto in violation of international humanitarian law" (U.S. Justice Buergenthal, in a separate declaration)—segments that comprise more than 80 percent of the wall. All irrelevant, since George Bush the "decider" has ruled that Israel can permanently keep the illegal settlements that are being protected by the Wall. Also irrelevant is the fact that as a High Contracting Party, the United States is obligated to enforce the Geneva conventions and punish those who violate them: itself, in this case.

The same ICJ ruling, of course, applies to everything to the east of the annexation wall as well, particularly to Israeli settlement programs in the Jordan Valley—an extremely important fact, though barely reported. These programs have been clearly designed to drive Palestinians out of the region in favor of Jewish settlement, thus imprisoning whatever scattered fragments are to be left to Palestinians.

As I write, Israeli troops and bulldozers have just demolished homes in more Jordan Valley villages, leaving sixty-five people homeless, along with another ten whose homes were demolished near the town of Qalqilya, almost entirely surrounded by the Wall so as to render it virtually uninhabitable. To consider another current case, the village of Fasayil in the Jordan Valley is right next door to the flourishing Israel settlement of Tomer. Fasayil, in contrast, is not flourishing. Its drinking water is rationed by the occupying authorities, it is not allowed to construct or repair roads, electricity is scheduled to be cut. There is no school in the village, so children have to walk miles along dangerous paths. The villagers have tried to build a school, but that is banned, because "the area is designated for Israeli farming," according to the Israeli Civil Administration. Nevertheless, the villagers have again been attempting to build a school, despite an injunction from the Israeli authorities to halt work. Since the crimes are masked by silence, we do not know the outcome. But we do know, if we choose to, that there is nothing unusual about Fasayil and Tomer. Rather, the paired towns are a microcosm of the West Bank—the reality of what we should call the U.S.-Israeli occupation, if we are honest.[24]

Israel continues to carry out its settlement programs, announcing, if questioned, that the territories "will remain in Israel's hands."[25] The programs in the Greater Jerusalem area violate Security Council resolutions dating back to 1968. Some of the new settlements surrounding Jerusalem are designated for religious settlers, "who will benefit from new homes at relatively inexpensive prices," thanks to robbery of Palestinian land and government subsidies. The "ultra-Orthodox ... constitute the fastest-growing portion of the settler population, according to figures from Peace Now and Israel's Central Bureau of Statistics." The United States "reacted by reminding Mr. Olmert that limiting settlement activity is a 'road-map obligation' Israel committed itself to as part of the Annapolis Process," probably eliciting a few chuckles in Tel Aviv and Jerusalem. The settlements have the multiple purposes of benefiting ultraorthodox settlers, extending the bounds of the (unchallengeably) Jewish state, improving Olmert's political prospects, and, crucially, cutting Palestinians off from the traditional center of their cultural, political, social, and economic life in Jerusalem.[26]

Highly visible violations of international law and the "Road Map" are sometimes reported, as are major atrocities. But not the traditional methods of reaching the intended goals, dating back to the origins of the Zionist project: "dunam after dunam," quietly, in the manner frankly explained by the dovish Shimon Peres administration in accord with the principles enunciated decades earlier by Moshe Dayan (See *Perilous Power*, pp. 179–180).

The "Annapolis Process" to which Washington's stern admonition referred is the series of peace talks that were planned at Annapolis, Maryland, in November 2007. A common and plausible interpretation is that the dramatic events were staged as part of the effort to line up the "moderate" Arab states, such as the Saudi tyranny, in Washington's crusade against Iran. Presumably there are other meeting places in the Washington area, but only one that is the base for the naval forces that are menacing Iran's coasts— a point that was presumably not lost on the participants and on Iran.

Some argue that, on its present course, Israel will become a pariah state like apartheid South Africa, with a large Palestinian population deprived of rights, laying the basis for a civil rights struggle for a unitary democratic state. That is dubious, however. Rather, the United States and Israel are likely to proceed exactly as they are now doing: quietly establishing the effective takeover of everything of value to them in the West Bank, including the Jordan Valley and the regions within the annexation wall, and carrying out massive infrastructure programs that leave Palestinians in unviable cantons. Gazans will be left to rot in desperation in the prison constructed for them, which Israel can use for target practice, sometimes resorting to violence to respond to—or, often, to incite—mindless criminal acts of rocket firing.[27] The contention of Gaza militants that the rockets are retaliation for continuing Israeli crimes in the West Bank, which Gazans accurately describe as inseparable from Gaza, is not even rejected in the West, because it is incomprehensible: How can anyone retaliate for actions supported by the leader of the Free World? Israel will take no responsibility for Palestinians who may somehow survive in the cantons that dot the West Bank landscape, far from the eyes of Israelis traveling on their segregated superhighways to their well-subsidized West Bank towns and suburbs, controlling the crucial water resources of the region, and benefiting from their ties with U.S. corporations that seem quite satisfied to see a loyal military power at the periphery of such a critical area, with an advanced high-tech economy offering them ample opportunities and benefits and with close links to Washington.

While systematically proceeding to undermine the basis for a viable two-state settlement in the West Bank, Israel can also turn to solving its internal "demographic problem," the presence of non-Jews in a Jewish state. The ultranationalist Knesset member Avigdor Lieberman was harshly condemned as a racist in Israel when he advanced the idea of forcing Israeli Arab citizens in the "triangle"—Wadi Ara—into a "Palestinian state," the population of course not consulted. One sign of the drift to the nationalist right in Israeli culture is that Lieberman's bitterly denounced proposal is slowly being incorporated into the mainstream. Knesset member Otniel Schneller of the governing party Kadima, "considered to be one of the people closest and most loyal to Prime Minister Ehud Olmert," proposed a plan that "appears very similar to one touted by Yisrael Beiteinu leader Avigdor Lieberman," though Schneller says his plan would be "more gradual," and the Arabs affected "will remain citizens of Israel even though their territory will belong to the [Palestinian Authority and] they will not be allowed to resettle in other areas of Israel." In December 2007, Foreign Minister Tzipi Livni, the last hope of many Israeli doves, adopted the same position. An eventual Palestinian state, she suggested, would "be the national answer to the Palestinians" in the territories and those "who live in different refugee camps or in Israel." With efficient PR, the forceful transfer of unwanted Arab citizens to a derisory "Palestinian state" could even be presented to the world as a generous "land swap."[28]

The basic line of argument was laid out decades ago by the respected humanist Michael Walzer, editor of the democratic socialist journal *Dissent*: "[N]ation building in new states is sure to be rough on groups marginal to the nation," he explained, and people of good will should appreciate that "the roughness can only be smoothed out ... by helping people to leave who have to leave"—in this case, the marginal people who are the remnants of what is now recognized to have been the "ethnic cleansing" of 1948.[29]

Once Israeli Arabs are dispatched to their natural place, Israel would have achieved the long-sought goal of freeing itself from the Arab taint—a stand that is familiar enough in U.S. history, for example in Thomas Jefferson's hope, never realized, that the rising empire of liberty would be free of "blot or mixture," red or black.

Livni is quoted in a rare report that slightly opens the door on why the Walzer-Lieberman-Schneller-Livni concerns are so important. Despite heroic efforts by apologists, it is not easy to conceal the fact that a "democratic Jewish state" is no more consistent with liberal principles than a "democratic" Christian, Muslim, or White state, as long as the blot or mixture is not removed. Such notions could be tolerated if the religious/ethnic identification were mostly symbolic, as when selecting an official day of rest. But in the case of Israel, it goes far beyond that. The most extreme departure from minimal democratic principles is the complex array of laws and bureaucratic arrangements designed to vest control of more than 90 percent of the land, including state land, in the hands of the Jewish National Fund (JNF), an organization committed to using charitable funds in ways that are "directly or indirectly beneficial to persons of Jewish religion, race or origin," so its documents explain: "a public institution recognized by the Government of Israel and the World Zionist Organization as the exclusive instrument for the development of Israel's lands," restricted to Jewish use in perpetuity, and barred to non-Jewish labor (though the principle is often ignored for imported cheap labor, and there are some marginal exceptions).[30]

This radical violation of elementary civil rights, funded by American citizens thanks to the tax-free status of the JNF, finally reached Israel's High Court in 2000, in a case brought by the highly assimilated middle-class Kaadan family, who had been barred from the all-Jewish town of Katzir near the Arab village where they lived (See *Perilous Power*, p. 160). The Court ruled in their favor. After an "11-year battle," and six years after the High Court ruling, the Kaadan family finally succeeded in buying a home in Katzir. They hope that their former home will be bought by a Jew, explaining that "[i]t's a known fact that the State of Israel takes care of every Jew, all over the world. As soon as a Jew moves in they'll give us new asphalt roads without potholes. The electricity network will be replaced too, and even the sewer system will be improved. And maybe, just maybe, they'll build a little synagogue, the light from which will finally enable us to see our way at night."[31]

The narrowly worded Court decision seems to have been barely implemented. Few cases are reported. Seven years later, a young Arab couple was barred from the town of Rakefet, on state land, on grounds of "social incompatibility."[32] Again, none of this is unfamiliar in the United States. After all, it took a century before the Fourteenth Amendment was even formally recognized by the courts, and it still is far from implemented.

Reflecting on recent and probably continuing U.S. policies, Israeli journalist and dovish political leader Yossi Sarid observed that U.S. "moral deterrence has vanished.... Any war criminal can scrub and launder his misdeeds with U.S. soap." It is a regular occurrence. Some of the illustrations are surreal. Thus Lithuania issued an arrest warrant for an "enemy combatant," borrowing from the Bush-Cheney-Rumsfeld lexicon, where the term applies to someone believed to be defending his country from foreign aggression. The target in this case was Yitzhak Arad, a partisan hero who went on to become an Israeli general and served for twenty years as head of the Holocaust museum Yad V'shem. Arad had "written openly and proudly of his contribution as a partisan to the liquidation of several ranking Lithuanian Nazi collaborators," Israeli commentator Reuven Kaminer writes, noting that "Lithuania was unique in that most of the Jews murdered in that country were victims of Lithuanian authorities." Lithuania approached Israel through diplomatic channels to get its hands on Arad. A few months later its Foreign Minister was welcomed to Israel on a state visit, meeting with President Shimon Peres and Foreign Minister Tsipi Livni, and was greeted with respect on a visit to Yad V'Shem, while relations remain just fine.[33]

What tomorrow will bring if matters proceed on their present course, one hates to think.

NOTES

This piece was originally published in the postscript of the paperback edition of Perilous Power: The Middle East and U.S. Foreign Policy *(Boulder, CO: Paradigm Publishers, 2009).*

1. See Benjamin Page with Marshall Bouton, *The Foreign Policy Disconnect* (Chicago: University of Chicago Press, 2006). The same is true of domestic policy. For many examples, see my *Failed States* (New York: Metropolitan Books, 2006).

2. Vicente Navarro, "Yes, We Can! Can We? The Next Failure of Health Care Reform," *Counterpunch Special Report*, March 6, 2008, available online at http://www.counterpunch.org/navarro03062008.html. Professor of Public Policy, Sociology, and Policy Studies at Johns Hopkins University, Navarro is one of the leading specialists on health care reform.

3. For useful analysis, see Mike Davis, *In Praise of Barbarians* (Chicago: Haymarket, 2007), Ch. 8.

4. Ibid. (emphasis in original). See also pp. 47f. of paperback edition of *Perilous Power*.

5. C. Chivers, "Grozny Journal: Nonstop to Chechnya: As War Ebbs, Flights Return," *New York Times*, September 11, 2007.

6. "Declaration of Principles for a Long-Term Relationship of Cooperation and Friendship Between the Republic of Iraq and the United States of America," signed on August 26, 2007, available online at http://www.whitehouse.gov/news/releases/2007/11/20071126-11.html; Charlie Savage, "In Signing Statement, Bush Looks to Bypass Four Laws," *Boston Globe*, January 29, 2008; Thom Shanker and Steven Lee Myers, "U.S. to Insist Iraq Grant It Wide Mandate in Operations," *New York Times*, January 25, 2008.

7. Kevin Ryan, "The 'Withdrawal' That Isn't," *Boston Globe*, March 29, 2007.

8. On vacillation, see Carolyn Lochhead, "Even If Dems Win, Total Exit Uncertain; Neither Clinton Nor Obama Promises to Pull Out All Troops," *San Francisco Chronicle*, March 17, 2008.

9. Taylor Owen and Ben Kiernan, "Bombs over Cambodia," *Walrus*, October 2006. Added to new edition. In a later reanalysis of the figures, Taylor and Kiernan conclude that the bombing of rural Cambodia, much of it "indiscriminate," was at or beyond the level of bombing in the entire Pacific Theater during World War II.

10. James Paul, quoted in "Five Years After Invading Iraq," Institute for Public Accuracy News Release, March 19, 2008, available online at http://www.accuracy.org/newsrelease.php?articleId=1672. For extensive background details, see Global Policy Forum, "War and Occupation in Iraq," June 2007, available online at http://www.globalpolicy.org/security/issues/iraq/occupation/report/index.htm.

11. Akiva Eldar, "Killing Yassin Saved Sharon," *Ha'aretz*, March 23, 2004; Brian Whitaker, "Assassination Method: Surveillance Drone and a Hellfire Missile," *Guardian*, March 23, 2004; and Palestinian Center for Human Rights, March 22, 2004, reporting seven civilians killed along with Yassin. For a review of Israel's assassination policies, see Tanya Reinhart, *The Road to Nowhere: Israel-Palestine Since 2003* (New York: Norton, 2006); and Victoria Brittain, "They Had to Die: Assassination Against Liberation," *Race and Class* 48, no. 1 (2006), p. 60. As Brittain observes, "With the beginning of the twenty-first century, Israeli assassination tactics became more violent, more reckless of the consequences for civilians and heedless of any international censure," thanks to U.S. protection, without which "Israel would long since have become the pariah state that apartheid South Africa became."

12. Pervez Hoodbhoy, "The War of Drones," *Dawn* (Pakistan), March 9, 2008.

13. CNN, February 1, 2008, transcript available online at http://edition.cnn.com/2008/US/01/31/alqaeda.death/index.html; Ethan Bronner, "Poll Shows Most Palestinians Favor Violence over Talks," *New York Times*, March 19, 2008; Steven Erlanger and Isabel Kershner, "Gunman in Jerusalem Attack Identified, *New York Times*, March 7, 2008.

14. Michael R. Gordon and Jeff Zeleny, "If Elected … Obama Envisions New Iran Approach," *New York Times*, November 2, 2007.

15. Program on International Policy Attitudes, "A Majority of Americans Reject Military Threats in Favor of Diplomacy with Iran," December 7, 2006, available online at http://www.worldpublicopinion.org/pipa/articles/brunitedstatescanadara/286.php.

16. Peter Grier, "Castro's Exit May Spur U.S. Policy Rethink," *Christian Science Monitor*, February 21, 2008.

17. Correlli Barnett, "Attack Iran and Spark World War," *Daily Mail* (London), March 4, 2007.

18. Cirincione quoted online at PIPA, "Iranians Want Capacity to Enrich Uranium But Accept NPT Rules Against Developing Nuclear Weapons," January 30, 2007, http://www.worldpublicopinion.org/pipa/articles/brmiddleeastnafricara/311.php.

19. PIPA, "American Public Says Government Leaders Should Pay Attention to Polls; Eight in Ten Say Public Should Have Greater Influence on Government," news release, March 21, 2008, available online at http://www.worldpublicopinion.org/pipa/articles/governance_bt/461.php.

20. Ibid.

21. The published parts of the NIE do not indicate that Iran had a nuclear weapons program prior to 2003. On reasons to question whether they did, see the interview with Iran specialist Ervand Abrahamian in David Barsamian, *Targeting Iran* (San Francisco: City Lights, 2007), pp. 86–87, citing high Iranian military officials. The critique by these officials of a nuclear program bears some similarity to the detailed argument by the prominent Israeli strategic analyst Zeev Maoz that Israel's nuclear weapons program has harmed its security. See *Defending the Holy Land* (Ann Arbor: University of Michigan Press, 2006).

22. Trita Parsi, *Treacherous Alliance: The Secret Dealings of Israel, Iran, and the United States* (New Haven, CT: Yale University Press, 2007).

23. Ismail Haniyeh, "Aggression Under False Pretenses," *Washington Post*, July 11, 2006; Khalid Mish'al, "Our Unity Can Now Pave the Way for Peace and Justice," *Guardian*, February 13, 2007.

24. News bulletin, Stop the Wall Campaign, March 11, 2008, available online at http://stopthewall.org/latestnews/1620.shtml; Rosie Walker, "Another Brick in the Wall: Saving Schools in the West Bank," *Independent* (U.K.), November 22, 2007.

25. Olmert quoted in Ilene Prusher, "Israel's 'Religious Right' Gains Clout, Complicating Peacemaking," *Christian Science Monitor*, March 19, 2008.

26. Prusher, "Israel's 'Religious Right' Gains Clout."

27. One index is provided by a Human Rights Watch report indicating that from September 2005, when Israeli settlers were transferred from Gaza to other occupied territories (called "withdrawal"), to late June 2006 (when Israeli attacks on Gaza sharply intensified), Israel fired more than 7,700 155-mm shells at northern Gaza. See Howard Friel and Richard Falk, *Israel-Palestine on Record* (New York: Verso, 2007).

28. "MK Schneller: Give PA Wadi Ara, 'Triangle,'" Israel National News, April 27, 2007; Livni quoted in Scott Wilson, "For Israel's Arab Citizens, Isolation and Exclusion," *Washington Post*, December 20, 2007.

29. See Michael Walzer, "Nationalism, Internationalism, and the Jews: The Chimera of a Binational State," in *Israel, the Arabs and the Middle East*, ed. Irving Howe and Carl Gershman (New York: Bantam 1972), a collection of democratic socialist essays. See also Benny Morris's interview with Ari Shavit in *Ha'aretz*, January 8, 2004. Morris, who has done some of the most important historical work refuting the traditional Zionist version of the events of 1948 and the subsequent conflict, believes that Ben-Gurion's greatest error in 1948, perhaps a "fatal mistake," was not to have "cleansed the whole country—the whole Land of Israel, as far as the Jordan River." The Hebrew phrase is "tihur etni," which translates literally as "ethnic purification."

30. Wilson, "For Israel's Arab Citizens." On the array of mechanisms, see my *Towards a New Cold War* (New York: Pantheon, 1982), and for more extensive analysis, Walter Lehn and Uri Davis, *The Jewish National Fund* (New York: Kegan Paul International, 1988). Some note that the JNF *owns* about an eighth of Israel's land, but the relevant figure is the amount of land it effectively *controls* and to which its discriminatory policies apply.

31. Yoav Stern, "Three-Story Home in Baka al-Garbiyeh for Sale; Jews Encouraged to Apply," *Ha'aretz*, May 1, 2006.

32. Wilson, "For Israel's Arab Citizens."

33. Yossi Sarid, *Ha'aretz*, November 11, 2006, quoted in Friel and Falk, *Israel-Palestine on Record*, p. 268; Reuven Kaminer, "Concern over Anti-Semitism," March 1, 2008, available online at http://groups.yahoo.com/group/JustPeaceUK/message/22794.

U.S. Foreign Policy in the Middle East

Delivered at UNESCO Palace
Beirut, Lebanon, May 25, 2010

It's very commonly agreed in foreign policy circles that
there are two major issues in American foreign policy today.
One of them is the threat of Iran, and the second one is the
unresolved Israel/Palestine conflict. Questions arise about
each of these issues. With regard to Iran, the first question
that arises is, "What, exactly, is the Iranian threat?" With
regard to Israel/Palestine, the obvious question is, "Why
isn't it resolved?" Actually, there are many problems in the
world where it's difficult even to imagine a solution, but
this one happens to be particularly easy. There is almost
universal agreement on what the solution should be, backed
by the Arab League; by the Organization of Islamic States,
including Iran; by Europe; by the United Nations; by international law; in fact, essentially by everyone. So how come
it isn't solved? That's the second question.

Well, there are some straightforward answers to these
questions, but they do not enter discussion within Western

ideology and doctrine, and the answers that are so simple are quite remote from general conventions. So let me say a few words about them.

With regard to the threat of Iran, there is a very authoritative answer, provided by military and intelligence reports to Congress in April 2010. They say that the threat of Iran is not a military threat. Iran has virtually no offensive military capacity. Its military spending is quite low, of course a minuscule fraction of U.S. military spending, but also pretty low by regional standards. They point out that the goal of Iranian military strategy is to try to defend the borders of the country and, in case they're attacked, to try to delay invading forces sufficiently so as to permit a negotiated settlement.

They discuss the question of whether Iran is developing nuclear weapons and say that, if they are developing nuclear weapons, which they don't know, the goal would be deterrence to prevent an attack on Iran. That's basically the story.

What then is the threat? Well, the threat is also explained. The primary threat is that Iran is engaged in destabilizing its neighbors. It's trying to increase its influence in surrounding countries, particularly in Iraq and Afghanistan. The U.S. is, of course, involved in Iraq and Afghanistan, but that is not destabilizing. That's stabilizing. The U.S. is there to improve stability and, if Iran tries to have influence in its neighboring countries, that's destabilizing. Now that's very standard terminology in foreign policy literature and discussion. I mean it reaches to the point that the former editor of *Foreign Affairs*, the main establishment journal, was able to say with a straight face and with no reaction from anyone that the United States had to destabilize Chile under Allende; had to destabilize the government of Chile, and overthrow it, and establish a dictatorship in order to bring about stability. It sounds like a contradiction, but it isn't when you understand that "stability" has a meaning. It means U.S. control. So we had to destabilize the country that was out of U.S. control in order to bring about stability, and it's the same problem with regard to Iran. It doesn't follow orders and, therefore, it is destabilizing the regional situation.

There is another problem with Iran; namely, it supports terrorism. So for example, you may believe today that you're celebrating National Liberation Day but, in terms of Western doctrine, what you're celebrating is the success of terrorism and, in fact, the success of aggression against Israel in Southern Lebanon ... Iranian aggression ... so you're celebrating Iranian aggression against Israel in Southern Lebanon and its success and celebrating terrorists and terrorism (quoting Israeli Labor Party high official Ephraim Sneh). It's not Liberation Day. You have to understand how to interpret these matters properly if you want to enter into the framework of imperial discourse. This is not just the U.S. and Israel. It's Western Europe as well. There are a few exceptions. So that's the threat of Iran.

The description is not incorrect. Iran does not follow orders. It's trying to maintain its sovereignty. This is all quite independent of what anyone thinks about its government. You may have the worst government in the world, but that's not the issue here. The U.S. doesn't care one way or the other what the government is like. It wants it to follow orders to improve stability. That's the Iranian threat.

What about Israel and Palestine? Well, there is an official version of that conflict, too. You see it every day in the newspapers. The United States is an honest broker and neutral arbiter trying to bring together two sides which are irrational and violent. They won't agree, and the United States is trying to settle the conflict between them. That's why there are proximity talks where the U.S. mediates between the two irrational opponents: the Palestinians and the Israelis. That's the official version. You can read it every day. There's also a reality. I won't run through the whole story, but the basic facts are clear.

In 1967, Israel conquered the Occupied Territories and there was a Security Council resolution calling for settlement of the conflict: UN 242. It called for Israel to withdraw to its borders and, in return, there should be guarantees for the security of every state in the region and recognition of every state in the region within recognized borders. There's nothing in it for the Palestinians. They are mentioned only as refugees. So that's in essence UN 242, which everyone agrees is the general framework for political settlement.

Well in 1971, four years later, President Sadat of Egypt offered Israel a full peace treaty, with nothing for the Palestinians. In return, total withdrawal from the occupied territories, and he really only cared about the Sinai. Jordan made a similar offer a year later. Israel had to make a decision. Are they going to choose security or expansion? A peace treaty with Egypt means security. Egypt was, of course, the major Arab military force. But they were, at that time, working hard to expand into Egyptian territory—into the Sinai, northeast Sinai, in order to establish a city and settlements and so on. They made what I think was the most fateful decision in the history of the country. They decided to prefer expansion to security, so they rejected the peace offer. Now the crucial question always is, "What is the Master going to do?" So, "What will Washington decide?" And there was a bureaucratic battle in Washington about this. Henry Kissinger won the internal battle and he was opposed to negotiations. He was in favor of what he called "stalemate," no negotiations. So he backed Israel's decision to choose expansion over security and that led very quickly to the 1973 war, the October War. It was a very close thing for Israel, and Israel and the United States recognized that they could not simply disregard Egypt. Then begins a long period of diplomatic interaction, ending up at Camp David a couple of years later, when the United States and Israel essentially accepted Sadat's 1971 proposal. This is called, in Western doctrine, a great diplomatic victory for President Carter and Henry Kissinger. In fact, it was a diplomatic catastrophe. They could have accepted it in 1971, and the cost of refusal was a very dangerous war and close to nuclear war; a lot of suffering and misery. Actually what the United States and Israel had to accept at Camp David was partially, from their point of view, harsher than Sadat's 1971 offer because, by this time, the issue of Palestinian national rights had entered the international agenda; so they had to accept, at least in words, some form of Palestinian national rights in the territories from which Israel was supposed to withdraw.

Meanwhile, in the intervening period, in 1976 there was another crucial event. In 1976, the major Arab states—Egypt, Syria, Jordan, and others—brought to the Security Council a resolution calling for a settlement of the conflict in terms of UN 242—all the relevant wording of 242 with its guarantees for rights and so on, but with an addition: a Palestinian state in the occupied territories. Israel refused to attend the session. The United States vetoed the resolution. It vetoed a similar one in 1980. Now when the United States vetoes a resolution, it's a double veto. First of all, it doesn't happen, and secondly, it's vetoed from history. So if you look at even the scholarly record it's rarely mentioned, and there certainly isn't anything in the media or general discussion. The events that I've just described didn't happen. They're not there. You have to search very hard to find a reference to them. That's one of the prerogatives of an imperial power. You can control history as long as you have a submissive intellectual class, which the West does have. I won't go through the rest of the history, but it continues pretty much like that.

Up to the present, the United States and Israel are out of the world. With rare and temporary exceptions, they have continued to block the political settlement that has almost universal agreement, which means that, if there were serious proximity talks today, conducted maybe from Mars, then the two antagonists that would be brought together would be the United States and the world. You could have proximity talks between them and, if they could reach an agreement, there would be a settlement of this problem. Well, that's the factual record.

Of course, historical events are always more complex than a simple description, but these are the basic facts. They're not controversial. There's no serious question about them, but they aren't part of general discourse about these topics because they lead to the wrong conclusions and, therefore, they're excluded. If I talk about this in the West in most places, the words are almost unintelligible. It's not unique to this case. It reveals the extraordinary power of imperial ideology. Even the simplest, the most obvious, the most crucial facts are invisible if they do not accord with the needs of power.

I'm by no means the first person to talk about this. George Orwell wrote about it, for example. He was discussing how in England, a free society, unpopular ideas can be suppressed without the use of force, just voluntarily, and he gave a few reasons. The most important one was a good education. He said, if you have a good education, you have instilled into you the understanding that there are certain things it wouldn't do to say—or even to think, for that matter. This essay of his is not very well known because it wasn't published, maybe proving his thesis. This was to be the introduction to his book *Animal Farm.* Everyone has read *Animal Farm.* It's about the totalitarian state, the totalitarian enemy and its evil ways. But, just to prevent too much self-satisfaction, Orwell wrote an introduction commenting on free England. It was not published. It was found many years later in his unpublished papers. It is not his greatest essay, but his point is basically correct. Unpopular ideas can be suppressed without the use of force, and a good education is an effective means to reach this result. Well, unless we can become capable of thinking the thoughts that are banned by imperial ideology, understanding of what's happening in the world is going to be very difficult to attain.

I'll come back to these two crucial issues of foreign policy, but first let me add a little background and what I think is appropriate context. The United States is, of course, the dominant force in world affairs and has been since the Second World War. It's very important to understand that there are a number of aspects of U.S. history which affect policy right to the present and I think are not sufficiently appreciated. One fact is that the United States is a settler-colonial society. Settler-colonialism is by far the worst kind of imperialism because it destroys or eliminates the native population. Part of the reason, I think, for the more or less reflexive sympathy for Israel in the United States is the recognition that Israel is pretty much reliving our history as a settler-colonial society. We got rid of an indigenous population, and Israel has been doing something similar.

There are lots of ironies involved in this. The original settlers regarded themselves as the children of Israel. They were returned to the Promised Land. They were united by a principle that runs through American history right up to the present. It's called Providentialism. We're fulfilling God's will. Whatever we do, we're fulfilling God's will. If we exterminate the natives, that must be God's will. We're trying to do good, of course; we're trying to be benevolent, but sometimes God's purposes are mysterious. You can read discussions by Supreme Court justices who were very surprised that the Indians were being exterminated—as they put it, were like withered leaves of autumn blowing away—and God's inscrutable will is leading to this unfortunate consequence. We are benevolent and work to improve their situation and to be nice to them, but they are somehow kind of withering away. That's Providentialism.

The State of Massachusetts was one of the first places settled by the English colonists. It got its charter in 1629 from the King of England. The charter was given to it with the purpose of benevolence to the indigenous population, helping the indigenous population, rescuing them from paganism. That was the goal of the commonwealth. In fact, the colony had a great seal with an image that depicts its goal. The image shows an Indian with a scroll coming out of his mouth and on the scroll it says, "Come over and help us." So, "Please come here and help us," and the colonists were trying to help them. Today that's called humanitarian intervention. They're coming to help them but, for some reason, they withered away like the leaves of autumn by God's inscrutable will which is beyond our understanding.

Well, another crucial fact about the United States is that it was founded as an empire, explicitly. The father of the country, George Washington, defined the United States as an infant empire, in his words, and his colleagues agreed. The most libertarian of the founding fathers, Thomas Jefferson, predicted that the newly liberated colonies would extend over the entire hemisphere. They would create a free hemisphere in which there would be no red, no black, and no Latin. The red—the Indians—would be driven away, or would wither away or disappear. The blacks were sort of needed for a while for slavery but, when slavery ends, they'll go back to where they belong to Africa and later Haiti. As for the Latins of the south, they're an inferior race so they will gradually be swept away by a superior race of Anglo-Saxons. To quote a major academic historian on this topic, Jefferson pictured the United States as the homeland for teeming millions who would immigrate and reproduce their kind in all parts of North and South America, displacing not only the indigenous red men but also the Latin population, creating a continent that would be American in blood, in language, in habits, and in political ideology. Well, that was the goal. It wasn't quite achieved but it was substantially achieved in one or another way. Through the 19th century, the United States established what is now called its national territory. That meant virtually exterminating the indigenous population as was recognized by the more honest leaders, by conquering half of Mexico, and various other not too pleasant actions.

Historians of imperialism sometimes talk about what they call the salt water fallacy. The salt water fallacy means it's called imperialism only if you cross salt water. So if the Mississippi River had been as wide as the Irish Sea, then it would have been imperialism but, since it's narrower, it's not called imperialism. But the people who carried out the conquest had no such illusions. They understood it to be imperialism whether it crossed salt water or not, and they were very proud of the imperial achievement in establishing the national territory.

By the end of the century, they were facing salt water and they expanded to conquer Cuba, Puerto Rico, Hawaii, and so on; and went on to conquer the Philippines, killing hundreds of thousands of people, but always with the most benevolent of intentions. It was just pure altruism. Tears come to your eyes in reading the odes to the benevolence of these conquests—features that are, again, almost universal in imperial practice. It's hard to find an imperial power that didn't put forth the same kind of posture.

By the First World War, it was beginning to be recognized that oil was going to be a fundamental commodity in the coming world picture, so Woodrow Wilson kicked the British out of Venezuela, a major oil producer, and took it over and supported a vicious dictator. That continued for a long period after Wilson. Within a few years, Venezuela was the biggest oil exporter in the world. The U.S. was the major producer, but Venezuela was the major exporter with U.S. corporations running it. And so it continued.

In the Middle East, it was recognized by the 1920s that it was a huge source of energy, so the U.S. did intervene there and managed to take part of the concession that was mostly British and French, but the U.S. was powerful enough to take control of part of the concession. During the Second World War, there was actually a small war going on between the United States and Britain to determine who would control Saudi Arabia. This was recognized as a future prize, and the U.S., of course, won that conflict and took it over.

Up until World War II, the United States was not a major player in world affairs. It controlled the Western Hemisphere and had some forays in the Pacific, but the major actors in world affairs were, primarily, Britain and, secondarily, France. But the Second World War changed all that. The United States had by far the largest economy in the world.

In fact that was true a century ago, but it was not the major actor in world affairs. World War II changed that, and it was clear that it was going to emerge from the war as the major world power. The planners in President Roosevelt's State Department and the Council on Foreign Affairs understood that. They had extensive meetings running right through the war, from 1939 to 1945, to plan the post-war world, a world in which the U.S. would be the dominant power. Their plans were quite important and, in fact, were implemented almost as they described them. The major concept that they developed was the concept of what they called the Grand Area. The Grand Area would be totally controlled by the United States. It would include the Western Hemisphere, of course; the entire Far East; and the former British Empire, including the Middle East energy resources. At least that much would have to be part of the Grand Area.

Now, in the early stages of the war, they assumed that Germany would emerge from the war as a major European power, so there would be two worlds: the U.S. world controlling the Grand Area, and the Germans controlling parts of Europe and Asia. By the time that the Russians started driving the Germans troops back after Stalingrad, it became clear that Germany was not going to survive the war, and the concept of the Grand Area was expanded to include as much of Eurasia as possible—at least the core, the economic, political, social, and economic core of Eurasia, mainly Western Europe, at least that. Actually, there were plans to go beyond. The British were, by 1943, beginning to plan for a post-war period in which the allies would immediately attack Russia and destroy it. Winston Churchill was particularly committed to this. In fact, in May 1945, when the war formally came to an end, and he ordered war plans for what was called Operation Unthinkable: the Wehrmacht, the German army, backed by the Royal Air Force and the American Air Force, would attack Russia and destroy it. It was never implemented, but that was the goal. The openly stated goal of the atom bomb was "to subdue the Russians." Those were the words of General Leslie Groves, who was in charge of the Manhattan Project that developed the bomb. In brief, we're going to subdue you, and you can't do anything about it.

There were hopes of expanding the Grand Area to a global area. Well, that didn't quite happen either, but it came pretty close.

What about the Middle East? It was understood that Middle East oil resources are critical for world control. One leading planner pointed out that control over Middle East oil would yield substantial control over the world. France was expelled from the region, the British were gradually reduced to a junior partner, and the U.S. emerged as the dominant force in controlling Middle East oil and, therefore, it was hoped, the world.

Now, Western Europe was part of the Grand Area, but it was always understood that sooner or later, Europe might pursue an independent path, perhaps following the Gaullist vision of Europe from the Atlantic to the Urals and something had to be done to prevent that. Well, a number of things were done. One of them was called NATO. One of its main purposes is to ensure that Europe will be contained within a U.S.–run military alliance. That leads to consequences right up to the moment. This concern that

Europe might become independent is sometimes tinged with a certain degree of contempt. Just a few days ago, in fact, the president of the Council on Foreign Relations (the main government foreign relations group), Richard Haass, wrote an article called, "Good-Bye Europe." Europe, he says, is no longer a high-ranking power in international affairs, and the reason is it's not violent enough. It's refusing to provide troops to control the world at an adequate level, so "Good-Bye Europe." It can sink into oblivion. No one really believes that, but that's in the background. Well, throughout the sort of official version of this whole period is called the Cold War. So what was the Cold War?

You can look at ideology or you can look at facts, at events. The events of the Cold War are very clear. The primary events of the Cold War were regular intervention and subversion within the Grand Area, always with the justification that we were defending ourselves from what John F. Kennedy called the "monolithic and ruthless conspiracy" to control the world, so that's why we have to intervene. The Russians did the same thing in their smaller domains. In fact, the Cold War was pretty much a tacit compact between the big superpower and the little superpower, in which each one was pretty much free to do what it wanted in its own domains, Russia in Eastern Europe, the U.S. everywhere else, appealing to the threat of the enemy. Sometimes it got out of control and came very close to terminal nuclear war but, basically, that was the Cold War structure.

There's another principle which ought to be borne in mind which is one of the major operative principles in world affairs right up to the present, and that is what we might call the Mafia principle. International affairs are run very much like the Mafia. The Godfather does not permit disobedience. That's actually fairly explicit in the Grand Area planning, although not in exactly those words.

In the Grand Area, the U.S. was to have "unquestioned power" with "military and economic supremacy" while ensuring "limitation of any exercise of sovereignty" by states that might interfere with its global designs. That's the Mafia principle. Actually, that's the Iranian threat. They're trying to exercise sovereignty, and that's not permitted under the Mafia principle. You can't permit independence. You must have obedience, and it's understandable. If somebody is disobedient, maybe some small country or, in the Mafia, some small storekeeper, if they get away with it, others may get the idea that they can do it, too, and pretty soon you have what Henry Kissinger called a virus that spreads contagion. If a virus might spread contagion, you have to kill the virus and inoculate everyone else by imposing brutal dictatorships and so on. That's a core part of Cold War history. If you look at it closely, you see that that's what it amounted to.

Well meanwhile, the Grand Area was becoming more diversified. In 1950, at the end of the Second World War, the United States literally had half the world's wealth and unimaginable security and power. By 1970, that had reduced to about 25 percent of the world's wealth, which is still colossal, but far less than 50 percent. The industrial countries had reconstructed, and decolonization had taken place. The world was becoming what was called tri-polar:

the U.S.–centered North American system, Europe based primarily on Germany and France, and the Japan–centered developing Northeast Asian economy. Today it's gotten more diversified. The structure is becoming more complex and much harder to control. Latin America, for the first time in its history, is moving towards a degree of independence. There are south/south contacts developing. Thus China now is Brazil's leading trading partner. Also, China is intruding into the crucial Middle East region and contracting and taking the oil.

There's a lot of discussion these days in foreign policy circles about a shift in power in the global system with China and India becoming the new great powers. That's not accurate. They are growing and developing, but they're very poor countries. They have enormous internal problems. There is, however, a global shift of power: it's from the global workforce to private capital. There's an Asian production center with China at the heart of it, largely an assembly plant for the surrounding more advanced Asian countries—Japan, Singapore, Taiwan, South Korea—which produce sophisticated technology, and parts and components, and send them to China where they're assembled and sent out to the United States and Europe. U.S. corporations are doing the same thing. They produce high-technology exports to China where they are assembled, and you buy them at home as an iPod or a computer, something like that. They're called Chinese exports, but that's quite misleading. You can see it very clearly if you look at the actual statistics. So there's a lot of concern about the U.S. debt. Well actually, most of the U.S. debt is held by Japan, not by

China. There's concern about the trade deficit. We purchase so much more from China than we export to them. Meanwhile, the trade deficit with Japan, South Korea, and Taiwan is going down. The reason is that Japan, South Korea, and Taiwan, and so forth are providing materials to China for them to assemble. These are counted in the United States as imports from China, but that's completely misleading. It's the Asian production center which is developing, and U.S. corporations and regional advanced economies are deeply involved in it. Meanwhile, the share of wealth of the workforce globally is declining. In fact, it is declining even faster in China, relative to the economy, than it is elsewhere. So when we look at the world realistically, there is a global shift of power, but it's not a shift to the Chinese/Indian power displacing the United States. It's a shift from working people all over the world to transnational capital. They are enriching themselves. It's essentially an old story, but it's taking new forms with the availability of the global workforce. Capital is mobile, and labor is not. It has obvious consequences.

Now all of this is fine for financial institutions, and corporate managers, and CEOs, and retail chains, but it is very harmful to populations. That's part of the reason for many significant social problems inside the United States. I don't have time to go into them.

To get some real insight into global policy, one place to look is at Grand Area planning during the Second World War and its implementation. Another place to look is at the end of the Cold War.

So what happened at the end of the Cold War? In 1989, when the wall fell and the Soviet Union collapsed, there was no more Cold War. What happened? The president of the United States at the time was George Bush, the first George Bush, and the Bush administration immediately produced new plans to deal with the post–Cold War system. The plans, in brief, were that everything would remain as it was before, but with new pretexts. So there still has to be a huge military force, but not to defend ourselves against the Russians because they are gone. Rather now, it was to defend ourselves—I'm quoting—against the "technological sophistication" of third-world powers. You're not supposed to laugh. That's what we need a huge military force for, and, if you're a well-educated person, following Orwell's principle, do not laugh. Say, "Yes, we need to defend ourselves from the technological sophistication of third-world powers." It was necessary to maintain what's called the "defense industrial base." That's a euphemism for high-tech industry. High-tech industry does not develop simply by free market principles. The corporate system can provide for more consumer choice, but high-tech develops substantially in the state sector: computers, the Internet, and so on. It's commonly been done under the pretext of defense. But with the Cold War over, we still have to maintain the "defense industrial base." That is the state goal: it is supporting high-tech industry.

What about intervention forces? Well, the major intervention forces are in the Middle East where the energy resources are. The post–Cold War plans said that we must maintain these intervention forces directed at the Middle

East, and then came an interesting phrase: where the serious problems "could not be laid at the Kremlin's door." The problems, in other words, were not caused by the Russians. So in other words, quietly, we have been lying to you for 50 years, but now the clouds have lifted and we have to tell the truth, in part at least. The problem was not the Russians all along. It was what is called radical nationalism, independent nationalism, which is seeking to exercise sovereignty and control their own resources. Now, that's intolerable all over the world because of the Mafia principle. You can't allow that. That's still there, so we still need the intervention forces. Same in Latin America, same everywhere, even though there are no Russians.

Well, what about NATO? That's an interesting case. If you believed anything you read during the Cold War years, you would have concluded that NATO should have disappeared. NATO was supposed to be there to protect Europe from the Russian hordes. OK? No more Russian hordes. What happens to NATO? Well, what happened to NATO was that it expanded. It's expanding more right now. The details are fairly well known. They're well studied by good scholarship. Gorbachev, the Russian premier, made a remarkable concession. He agreed to let a unified Germany join NATO, a hostile military alliance. It's quite remarkable. Germany alone had virtually destroyed Russia twice in a century. Now, he was allowing it to rearm in a military alliance with the United States. Of course there was a quid pro quo. He thought that there was an agreement that NATO would become a more political organization. In fact, he was promised that by the Bush administration. NATO would be more of a political organization and it would not expand "one inch to the East." That was the phrase that was used. It would not expand into East Germany or certainly not beyond. Well, Gorbachev was naïve. He accepted that agreement. He didn't realize that the Bush administration had not put it into writing. It was just a verbal agreement, a gentleman's agreement, and, if you have any sense, you don't make gentlemen's agreements with violent superpowers. Gorbachev was quite upset when he discovered that the agreement was worthless. When NATO began immediately to expand into the East, he brought up the agreement, and Washington pointed out that there's nothing on paper, which is true. There was nothing on paper. It was a gentleman's agreement. NATO expanded to the East. It expanded into East Germany very quickly and, in the Clinton years, it expanded even further into Eastern Europe; later much more. By now, the secretary general of NATO explains that NATO must expand further still. NATO must take responsibility for controlling the entire global energy system—that means pipelines, sea lanes, and sources.

Just a few weeks ago, there was an international meeting headed by Madeleine Albright, secretary of state under Clinton. They issued plans called NATO 2020, and they said NATO must be prepared to operate far beyond its borders without limit, meaning it must become a worldwide U.S. military intervention force. So that's NATO, no longer there to defend ourselves from the Russians, but their real purpose is to control the whole world.

Well, let me say a few words about the Israeli/Palestine conflict, which developed within this context. I've said a few words about the history. The basic record is one of almost total U.S. rejectionism, its refusal to join the overall accepting of a political settlement which makes sense. There's been one important exception, a very interesting exception. At the end of his term, in the year 2000, Clinton recognized that the proposals that he and Israel had put forth at Camp David had failed. He recognized that those would never be acceptable to any Palestinians so he, therefore, changed the proposals. In December of 2000, he produced what he called his parameters, a general framework for agreement. It was vague, but it was more forthcoming. He then gave a speech in which he said that both sides had accepted the parameters, and both sides had expressed reservations. They then met, Israel and Palestine, in Taba, Egypt, in January to try to work out their disagreements, and they came very close to a total settlement. In their last press conference, jointly they said that with a little more time, they could have reached complete settlement. Well, Israel terminated the negotiations, and that was the end of that.

That tells you something. It tells you that with the U.S. pressing both sides to join the world to permit a political settlement, pretty much along the lines of the international consensus, it can happen. A lot has taken place since 2001, but I think those principles remain. I think it's quite striking to see how people who write the history deal with this. So one of the main books about the negotiations is by Dennis Ross, Clinton's chief negotiator. He gives a detailed account of all the efforts of the United States, the neutral arbiter, the honest broker, to bring the two sides together and he concludes, in the end, it failed and it was all the fault of the Palestinians. They reject everything. Ross is very careful to end this book in December of 2000, just before his primary thesis was completely refuted. It was completely refuted a few weeks later. He ended the book there, and commentators don't say anything about it. That's discipline. If you want to be a respected intellectual, you have to understand these things. You do not expose power, especially if you hope to join the academic world or diplomacy. So Ross terminates the book before the thesis is refuted, and that's accepted and is now our history, excluding the crucial reality, just as in the case of the earlier events that I've described thus far. But in reality it's there and that still goes on until today. So what does that leave for options for today for the Palestinians and those concerned with Palestinian rights?

One option is that the United States will join the world as it did for a couple of weeks in January 2001, and we'll agree to some version of the international consensus, something like the Taba agreements. Now there's a very common view expressed by many Palestinian groups and by many others that are sympathetic with them, holding that that's not a possibility and that there's a better alternative. The better alternative that they're proposing would be for Palestinian leaders to say that we'll give the key to Israel, and they'll take it. We'll give them all the occupied territories and then there will be a civil-rights struggle, an internal anti-apartheid struggle, and a struggle like that can be won and we'll get somewhere. There are a lot of quite good people proposing this, but they are failing to notice that there is a third alternative. A third alternative is that the U.S.

and Israel will continue doing exactly what they're doing, meaning a version of what Ehud Olmert, when he was prime minister, called *convergence.* Israel takes over everything within what they call the separation wall, well, actually an annexation wall. They take over the water resources, the valuable land, the suburbs of Jerusalem and Tel Aviv, and so on. Israel also takes over what is called Jerusalem, which is actually the huge area of Greater Jerusalem. It takes over the Jordan Valley—more arable land. And then it sends corridors through the remaining regions to break them up into separated cantons. So there's one east of Jerusalem, almost to Jericho, virtually bisecting the West Bank, there are separate ones further north.

Now, what about the Palestinians? They are just left out of this. Very few will be incorporated in the valuable areas that Israel will take over, so there won't be any civil-rights struggle. There won't be what's called a "demographic problem": too many Arabs in a Jewish state. The rest of the Palestinians will leave or will be left to rot in the hills, apart from a privileged elite. They're not part of what Israel is taking over. What's left to the Palestinians they can do whatever they want with. If they want to call it a state, then fine, call it a state. In fact, the first prime minister to make this proposal was Netanyahu. He's the first Israeli prime minister to say, "Yes, there can be a Palestinian state"— that was in 1996. He came into office in 1996. He replaced Shimon Peres. As Peres left office, he said that there will never be a Palestinian state. Netanyahu came in, and his administration said, "Well, Palestinians can call whatever fragments are left to them a state if they want or they can call them 'fried chicken.'" That comes right up to the present. Just a few weeks ago, Silvan Shalom, who is the vice premier and the regional development minister, responded to Palestinian initiatives about creating the basis for a state, and when asked what he thought about it, he said, "That's fine if they want to call what we leave them a state; that's fine. It will be a state without borders just like Israel, also a state without borders. Of course, we will have everything of value, and they will have fried chicken, but that's OK, and that should stop the pressure against us for a diplomatic settlement, and everything will be wonderful."

Well, that's an improvement over the past. If you go back to say 1990, the position of the Israeli government and the U.S. government, James Baker and George Bush, was that the Palestinians do have a state, namely Jordan, and they cannot have an additional Palestinian state. That was the official position since 1990. Now, it's slightly improved. The U.S. and Israel agree that Jordan isn't a Palestinian state, and the Palestinians can have fried chicken, fragments of territory which the U.S. and Israel will assign. Now that's the alternative.

What about the civil-rights struggle, the anti-apartheid struggle? That's not an alternative. The operative choices are a two-state settlement in accord with the international consensus and international law, perhaps along the lines almost reached at Taba; or "fried chicken" while Israel takes what it wants, as it can, as long as it has unfailing U.S. support.

Well, I will finish by saying just one word about the likely prospects. There are many analogies made between Israel and South Africa. Most of them are pretty dubious, I think. For example, Ariel Sharon, the architect of the settlement policy, called the fragments to be left to the Palestinians "Bantustans," as in the South African apartheid state. But these are not Bantustans. That's misleading. It's much worse than South Africa. White South Africa needed the black population. That was their workforce. Eighty-five percent of the population were blacks, so they had to take care of them just the way slave owners had to take care of slaves, and so the extreme South African racists provided some support for the Bantustans. In contrast, Israel does not need the Palestinians, doesn't want them. So if they wither away like the leaves of autumn, the way the Native Americans did, then that's fine. If they go somewhere else, that's fine. They're not going to take any responsibility for them. They don't need them. So it's worse than apartheid. They're not Bantustans. That analogy doesn't work, and many others don't, either, but there is one analogy that I think is correct, and it never seems to be discussed.

Fifty years ago, white South Africa was beginning to recognize that it was becoming a pariah state. It was being isolated from the world. It was getting less support. It was increasingly hated by everyone. At that point, the South African foreign minister spoke to the American ambassador in South Africa, and he pointed out to him that in the United Nations everyone's voting against us but it doesn't matter because you and I both know that there's only one vote in the United Nations. That's yours, and as long as you back us up, it doesn't matter what the world thinks. That's a recognition of the Mafia principle, realism in world affairs, and he proved to be correct. If you look at what happened in the following decades, opposition to South Africa continued to grow and develop. By about 1980, there was a sanctions and divestment campaign. Western corporations began pulling out. Sanctions were imposed by the U.S. Congress. But nothing changed. The reason was that Washington kept supporting South Africa. Ronald Reagan, who was president, violated the congressional sanctions for a reason: the war on terror that he declared on coming into office in 1981. He was conducting his war on terror, and South African whites were under threat of terror from the African National Congress, Nelson Mandela's ANC. In 1988, Washington declared the ANC to be one of the "more notorious terrorist groups" in the world. It really didn't matter what the rest of the world thought; in fact, even what the American people thought, or what Congress thought. If you don't like it, that's fine, but we're going to keep on and, by that time, the late 1980s, white South Africa looked absolutely impregnable. They had won military victories and were becoming richer. Everything looked fine, and they were very satisfied. Two or three years later, the United States changed its policy, and apartheid collapsed. When the godfather changes his policy, things change. The outcome is not very beautiful, but it was undoubtedly a major victory to eliminate apartheid, though there is still a long way to go. Nelson Mandela also won a personal victory, a bit more slowly. He was removed from Washington's list of people supporting terror only a year ago, so for the past year he's been able to travel to the United States without a special dispensation.

Essentially that's what happened, and I think this could happen with Israel. If the United States changes policy and decides to join the world, Israel will have no option but to go along. That shouldn't be the end of the line, any more than ending apartheid is the end of the line for South Africa. I have always believed and still think there are better solutions than the international consensus on a two-state settlement, but in the real world, that is probably an indispensible first step to any future progress towards a more just outcome.

Now, there is, as I mentioned, a good deal of complexity in the international system. There are organizations developing that are independent of the United States. There are countries that are maintaining their own sovereignty like China, for example, and there is a good deal of diversification. There are even steps towards a degree of independence within the U.S.-dominated domains. Take Egypt, the second largest recipient of U.S. military aid, after Israel. There were meetings a couple of weeks ago about nuclear proliferation, international meetings. Egypt, speaking for the 118 states of the nonaligned movement, took a very strong and principled stand on a crucial issue: establishing a nuclear weapons–free zone in the Middle East. Well, that is very hard for anyone to object to in principle. It would mitigate or end whatever potential nuclear threat is posed by Iran, supposedly the main U.S. foreign policy concern. Of course, it would have to involve Israel and U.S. forces in the region so the U.S. was kind of stuck. They can't come out against it, but they couldn't come out in favor of it, so they formulated a way to evade the dilemma, counting on the intellectual classes to conceal what was happening, following Orwell's principle. The Obama administration stated its support for a nuclear weapons–free zone, but said that this isn't the right time for it. We have to wait until there is a comprehensive peace settlement. But that can be delayed indefinitely by U.S.-Israeli rejectionism, as in the past, so the threat of a nuclear weapons–free zone can be delayed indefinitely, too. So far, Washington has gotten away with this, but the issue can be pressed by popular movements that take an independent stance.

Now, there are many other points where the prevailing system of domination, though powerful, is nevertheless vulnerable. There are many possibilities open to people to influence and determine the fate of the future.

Address to the United National Antiwar Conference

July 23–25, 2010, Albany, New York

I'm very pleased to have an opportunity to say a few words at the Albany United National Antiwar Conference and am sorry that circumstances make it impossible for me to be there with you in person.

There's no need to stress the significance of the task you are undertaking or the scale of the challenge. We all know that very well. The U.S. spends about as much on war and preparation for war as the rest of the world combined, and is technologically far more advanced, with plans on the books for future wars that range from tiny drones that can murder people in their living rooms to space platforms for near-instantaneous and massively destructive attack anywhere in the world. It is also responsible for 70 percent of arms sales and under Bush II was alone in barring a global treaty regulating the global arms trade. For accuracy, it was not quite alone: in 2008 the U.S. was joined by Zimbabwe. Apparently too embarrassing to merit reporting.

The U.S. is now fighting two wars of aggression in Asia and is planning a third. Military spending is escalating to unprecedented heights under Obama. Much concern is being whipped up about the deficit. Let's put aside the fact that we *should* be running a deficit to grow out of the economic catastrophe caused by the financial institutions that are now charged with putting Band-aids on the cancer for which they are primarily responsible, along with their representatives in Washington. Taking the deficit seriously, about half is due to military spending, and the rest is mostly due to the hopelessly inefficient and costly health care system imposed by the same hands. But the obvious ways to deal with the deficit are off the agenda. Rather, attention must be focused on depriving poor people of their meager benefits.

Considerations such as these are serious enough for those who care about this country, but they are of course marginal in comparison to the costs to the victims of our dedication to criminal violence. I'll omit the horrifying details, which are familiar to all of us.

I happen to be speaking almost a month before you are meeting in Albany, and the current pace of events is so fast that what I say is almost sure to be outdated by the time you meet, at least in part. I am speaking shortly after the McChrystal fiasco and the installation of his superior, General Petraeus, as his replacement. It is generally and plausibly assumed that among the consequences will be relaxation of the rules of engagement so that it becomes easier to kill civilians and extend the war well into the future, as Petraeus uses his considerable clout in Congress to achieve this result.

The same may well be true of the war in Iraq. I won't run through the ugly history, but will only mention one crucial feature of the war. The U.S. invaders were compelled to retreat step by step from their initial war aims, a major triumph of mass nonviolent resistance. The invaders were good at killing insurgents, but could not deal with hundreds of thousands demonstrating for elections that the occupying authorities sought desperately to avoid and then to subvert. These facts are, of course, denied by apologists, but they are understood by the most serious analysts like Jonathan Steele. The title of Steele's important book on the war is *Defeat*, accurately.

As the U.S. was forced to back down, war aims came to be stated with greater clarity. The usual boilerplate about democracy did not suffice as Washington sought to hang on in the face of Iraqi resistance and domestic opposition to the war. In November 2007, the Bush administration issued a Declaration of Principles for the U.S. and the Iraqi government. The Declaration states that U.S. forces are to remain indefinitely in Iraq and commits Iraq to facilitate and encourage "the flow of foreign investments to Iraq, especially American investments."

This brazen expression of imperial will was underscored when Bush quietly issued yet another signing statement a few months later, declaring that he will reject crucial provisions of congressional legislation that he had just signed, including the provision that forbids spending taxpayer money "to establish any military installation or base for the purpose of providing for the permanent stationing of United States Armed Forces in Iraq" or "to exercise United States control of the oil resources of Iraq." Nothing like that will be tolerated, even if passed by Congress and signed by the President. That's January 2008.

That was a last gasp. Shortly after, the Bush administration was compelled to sign a SOFA eliminating all of these demands. At least formally, the U.S. is committed to withdraw its forces in 2011 and U.S. firms have not done well in the competition for Iraqi resources. But I stress "formally." There is very little reporting from Iraq, and information is sparse. It does appear, however, that construction of the huge U.S. military bases is continuing, and Obama has budgeted a substantial increase for the huge U.S. embassy in Baghdad, actually a city within a city; Obama has similar plans for Islamabad and Kabul. All of this indicates plans for a long stay with a heavy footprint.

As if two wars in the region are not enough, Obama is now building up for a third: against Iran, which is widely regarded as posing the most severe crisis facing the U.S. Congress has just strengthened the sanctions against Iran. Obama has been rapidly expanding U.S. offensive capacity in the African island of Diego Garcia, claimed by Britain, which had expelled the population so that the U.S. could build the massive base it uses for attacking the Middle East and Central Asia. The Navy is expanding facilities for nuclear-powered, guided-missile submarines with Tomahawk missiles, which can carry nuclear warheads. Each submarine is reported to have the striking power of a typical carrier battle group. The Obama build-up also includes hundreds of "bunker buster" bombs, the most powerful in the arsenal short of nuclear weapons, intended for blasting hardened underground structures. Planning for these bombs began under Bush, but languished. Obama accelerated it sharply as soon as he took office, and they are now to be deployed years ahead of schedule—aimed, of course, at Iran.

The respected British strategic analyst Dan Plesch observes that "They are gearing up totally for the destruction of Iran. U.S. bombers and long range missiles are ready today to destroy 10,000 targets in Iran in a few hours. The firepower of U.S. forces has quadrupled since 2003," accelerating under Obama.

A U.S. fleet (with an Israeli vessel) is reported to have passed through the Suez Canal on the way to the Persian Gulf, where its task is "to implement the sanctions against Iran and supervise the ships going to and from Iran," according to Arab press reports. Chairman of the Joint Chiefs Admiral Michael Mullen visited Afghanistan a few days before I'm speaking. On his return, he went to Israel to meet senior military officials and planners. The main Israeli newspaper, *Haaretz*, reports that the meeting focused "on the preparation by both Israel and the U.S. for the possibility of a nuclear capable Iran." It has barely been reported here, like most of what I've just reviewed, although—or perhaps because—it is plainly of extreme significance and urgency.

The increasing threats of military action against Iran are, of course, in violation of the UN Charter and in specific violation of Security Council resolution 1887 of September 2009, which reaffirmed the call to all states to resolve disputes related to nuclear issues peacefully, in accordance with the Charter, which bans the use *or threat* of force.

What exactly is the Iranian threat? There are many apocalyptic pronouncements, but not descending to the level of evidence or sane argument. An authoritative answer is provided by in a government report to Congress on the military threat of Iran, in April. The brutal clerical regime is doubtless a threat to its own people, though it does not rank particularly high in that respect in comparison to

U.S. allies in the region. But that is not what concerns the report. Rather, it is concerned with the threat Iran poses to the region and the world.

The study makes it clear that the Iranian threat is not military. Iran's military spending is "relatively low compared to the rest of the region," and miniscule as compared to that of the U.S. Iranian military doctrine is strictly "defensive ... designed to slow an invasion and force a diplomatic solution to hostilities." Iran has only "a limited capability to project force beyond its borders." With regard to the nuclear option, "Iran's nuclear program and its willingness to keep open the possibility of developing nuclear weapons is a central part of its deterrent strategy."

Though the Iranian threat is not military, that does not mean that it might be tolerable to Washington. Iranian deterrent capacity is an illegitimate exercise of sovereignty that interferes with U.S. global designs. Specifically, it threatens U.S. control of Middle East energy resources, a high priority of planners since World War II, which yields "substantial control of the world," one influential liberal democrat advised 60 years ago, expressing a common understanding.

But Iran's threat goes beyond deterrence. It is also seeking to expand its influence. Iran is "destabilizing" the region. U.S. invasion and military occupation of Iran's neighbors is "stabilization." Iran's efforts to extend its influence in neighboring countries is "destabilization," hence plainly illegitimate. Normal usage, incidentally.

Beyond the crimes of deterrence and trying to establish friendly relations with neighbors, Iran is also supporting

terrorism, the government report continues: by backing
Hezbollah and Hamas, the major political forces in Lebanon and in Palestine—if elections matter, in this case the
only relatively free elections in the Arab world. It is normal
for elite opinion to fear the threat of democracy and to act
to deter it, but this is a rather striking case, particularly
alongside of strong U.S. support for the brutal regional
dictatorships. There is much more to say about the terrorist acts attributed to Hamas and Hezbollah, which pale in
comparison to U.S.-Israeli terrorism in the same region and
are largely resistant to U.S.-Israeli aggression and violence.
And could easily be terminated if the U.S. and Israel would
accept ceasefires and political settlement instead of prefer-
ring violence, brutal repression, and expansion, which they
recognize to be in violation of international law and even
specific Security Council resolutions.

The model for democracy in the Muslim world, despite
serious flaws, is Turkey, which has relatively free elections and has also been subject to harsh criticism in the
U.S. The Obama administration was particularly incensed
when Turkey joined with Brazil in arranging a deal with
Iran to restrict its enrichment of uranium, rather along the
lines that the U.S. had demanded. Obama had praised the
initiative in a letter to Brazil's president, Lula da Silva, apparently on the assumption that it would fail and provide
a propaganda weapon against Iran. When it succeeded, the
U.S. was furious, and quickly undermined it by ramming
through a Security Council resolution that was so meaningless that China cheerfully joined at once—recognizing
that at most the limited sanctions would impede Western

interests in competing with China for Iran's resources. Once again, Washington acted forthrightly to ensure that others would not interfere with U.S. control of the region, whatever the effect on proliferation.

The political class understands very well the threat of independent action. Steven Cook, a scholar with the Council on Foreign Relations, observed that the critical question now is "How do we keep the Turks in their lane?"—following orders like good democrats. A *New York Times* headline captured the general mood: "Iran Deal Seen as Spot on Brazilian Leader's Legacy." In brief, do what we say, or else. Any Mafia Don can explain.

There is no indication that other countries in the region favor U.S. sanctions any more than Turkey does. On Iran's opposite border, Pakistan and Iran have signed an agreement for a new pipeline. Even more worrisome for the U.S. is that the pipeline might extend to India. The 2008 U.S. treaty with India supporting its nuclear programs—and indirectly its nuclear weapons programs—was pretty clearly intended to stop India from joining the pipeline. India and Pakistan are two of the three nuclear powers that have refused to sign the Non-proliferation Treaty (NPT); the third being Israel. All have developed nuclear weapons with U.S. support, and still do.

No sane person wants Iran to develop nuclear weapons; or anyone. One obvious way to mitigate or eliminate this threat is to establish a nuclear weapons–free zone (NWFZ) in the Middle East. The issue arose (again) at the NPT conference at United Nations headquarters in early May 2010. Egypt, as chair of the 118 nations of the Non-Aligned

Movement, proposed that the conference back a plan calling for the start of negotiations in 2011 on a Middle East NWFZ, as had been agreed by the West, including the U.S., at the 1995 review conference on the NPT.

Washington still formally agrees, but insists that Israel be exempted—and has given no hint of allowing such provisions to apply to itself. The time is not yet ripe for creating the zone, Secretary of State Hillary Clinton stated at the NPT conference in May. Washington also insisted that no proposal can be accepted that calls for Israel's nuclear program to be placed under the auspices of the IAEA—as the IAEA is now advocating—or that calls on signers of the NPT, specifically Washington, to release information about "Israeli nuclear facilities and activities, including information pertaining to previous nuclear transfers to Israel." Obama's technique of evasion is to adopt Israel's position that any such proposal must be conditional on a comprehensive peace settlement, which the U.S. can delay indefinitely, as it has been doing for 35 years, with rare and temporary exceptions.

Obama's rhetorical commitment to nonproliferation has received much praise, even a Nobel peace prize. One practical step in this direction is establishment of NFWZs. Another is withdrawing support for the nuclear programs of the three nonsigners of the NPT. As often, rhetoric and actions are hardly aligned, in fact are in direct contradiction in this case, facts that pass with little attention.

Instead of taking practical steps towards reducing the truly dire threat of nuclear weapons proliferation, the U.S. is proceeding to take major steps towards reinforcing U.S. control of the vital Middle East oil-producing regions, by violence if other means do not succeed, with very ugly prospects.

Let's turn finally to Obama's major current war: Afghanistan. The official goal is to protect ourselves from Al Qaeda, which is a virtual organization with no specific base—a "network of networks" and "leaderless resistance," as it's been called in the professional literature, now even more so than before, with relatively independent factions, loosely associated, throughout the world. The CIA estimates that 50–100 Al Qaeda activists may now be in Afghanistan, and there is no indication that the Taliban want to repeat the mistake of offering sanctuary to Al Qaeda.

In the first exercise of Obama's new strategy, U.S. Marines recently conquered Marja, a small town in Helmand province, the main center of the insurgency. The *New York Times* reports that

> the Marines have collided with a Taliban identity so dominant that the movement appears more akin to the only political organization in a one-party town, with an influence that touches everyone. "We've got to re-evaluate our definition of the word 'enemy,'" said Brig. Gen. Larry Nicholson, commander of the Marine expeditionary brigade in Helmand Province. "Most people here identify themselves as Taliban. … We have to readjust our thinking so we're not trying to chase the Taliban out of Marja, we're trying to chase the enemy out," he said.

The Marines are facing a problem that has always bedeviled conquerors, one that is very familiar to the U.S.

from Vietnam, where the leading U.S. government scholar lamented that the enemy was the only "truly mass-based political party in South Vietnam" and any effort to compete with it politically would be like a conflict between a minnow and a whale: our minnow, their whale. Therefore, the U.S. had to overcome the indigenous enemy's political force by using its comparative advantage, violence—with horrifying results. Others have faced similar problems: for example the Russians in Afghanistan in the 1980s, where they won every battle but lost the war—though they were beginning to make progress, the top U.S. experts recognize, after they adopted the now fashionable Petraeus COIN strategy in the mid-80s. And they might have won, the same experts agree, had it not been for the massive support for the Mujahadeen by the U.S., Saudi Arabia, and Pakistan, including high-tech weapons that neutralized Russian helicopter forces. The CIA proudly proclaimed that the goal was not to liberate Afghanistan, but to kill Russians. The U.S. faces no such opposition in Afghanistan.

After the Marja triumph, the U.S.-led forces were poised to assault the major city of Kandahar, where, according to U.S. army polls, the military operation is opposed by 95 percent of the population, and 5 out of 6 regard the Taliban as "our Afghan brothers"—again, echoes of earlier conquests. The plans were delayed, part of the background for the McChrystal fiasco.

Under these circumstances, it is not surprising that the authorities are concerned that domestic public support may erode even further. A recently leaked CIA memorandum observes that "The Afghanistan mission's low public salience has allowed French and German leaders to disregard popular opposition and steadily increase their troop contributions" to the U.S. war, despite the opposition of 80 percent of the German and French publics. It is therefore necessary to "tailor messaging" to "forestall or at least contain backlash." Specific proposals follow for deluding the public. Here the media can be counted on to fulfill the needed role voluntarily.

The CIA memorandum should remind us that states have an internal enemy: their own population, which must be controlled when state policy is opposed by the public. The battle to control the internal enemy is highly pertinent today and should be a prime concern for those who hope to confront today's severe challenges, as you are now doing. Your task could hardly be more important.

Index

About the Author

Noam Chomsky, Professor of Linguistics at the Massachusetts Institute of Technology, is the author recently of *Hopes and Prospects* (2010) and *Perilous Power* (Paradigm 2007). His articles and books revolutionized the contemporary study of linguistics and his political writings are widely read and translated throughout the world. In 2003 a profile of Chomsky in the *New Yorker* described his influence as one of the most cited scholars in history.